To Mothers Raising Sons:

How to Love Them to Life

Instead of Death

by Kathei McCoy

Life Chronicles Publishing
Give your life a voice!

http://www.mylifechronicles.org

Life Chronicles Publishing
ISBN-13: 978-0998911403
ISBN-10: 0998911402

Cover Design:

Adrian Sims

Photo Credit:

Eyemagination Imaging

Life Chronicles Publishing Copyright © 2017

All rights reserved. No part of this book may be reproduced in any form or by any electronic or mechanical means, including information storage and retrieval systems, with or without permission from the publisher or author, except in the case of a reviewer, who may quote brief passages embodied in critical articles or in a review.

Dedication

This book is dedicated to the memory of my only child K'Breyan "KB" Clark who was murdered on March 29, 2013.

The moment you were born, I made a decision to free myself of the life I was living that felt meaningless, fruitless and kept me spinning my wheels.

The moment you died I made a decision to live

and not just be content with what was.

It was that decision that led me to discover my true freedom.

KB your life changed my life, and for the short 19 years you graced me with your presence, you were my reason for living.

In your death, you are still my reason for living.

I will spend the rest of my life showing others how to live instead of merely existing.

I love you to infinity and beyond!

Until we meet again my sweet prince, sweet dreams!

Table of Contents

Dedication

Introduction...3

Author's Notes...9

Part I – The Early Years

    Chapter 1 – The Frankenstein Syndrome.........................17

    Chapter 2 – Working for His Love....................................35

    Chapter 3 – The Boyfriend/Husband Replacement 67

Part II – The Tumultuous Teenage Years

    Chapter 4 – Rebellion..75

    Chapter 5 – Falling out of Love with Your Son..................93

    Chapter 6 – Loving Him When You Don't Like Him..........99

    Chapter 7 – Setting Boundaries......................................115

Part III – Turning Tragedy into Triumph

    Chapter 8 – Life After Loss..127

    Chapter 9 – The Struggle..135

    Chapter 10 – Moving Forward.......................................151

To Mothers Raising Sons

Introduction

Mothers, it's time for us to save our sons. Our sons are in trouble. The alarms are going off. We can no longer push the snooze button and wait for someone else do something about the dire state of emergency our boys are in. I am writing to you in love, as a mother who "gets" it, and to shine a light on what might be uncomfortable for some. This book shines light on what isn't being said, what's being avoided, what's being denied, and what is being swept under the rug. It is time to shine the light of truth on what is hard to hear and what is hard to face.

We've gotten too comfortable with passing blame, too comfortable with ignoring what's right in our faces and too comfortable with sugar coating the truth. It's this feeling of overwhelm and not knowing what to do that continues the cycle of our sons being lost to the streets, incarcerated, drug addicted and dying way too young. It's this complacency that has us spinning in the cycle of insanity; doing the same thing yet expecting different results. It is time for a deep and profound change within ourselves first, as mothers of sons, and in how we're raising our sons.

As a mother whose son was killed at the young age of 19, I know all too well the pain of losing a child. I want to speak truth and love regarding a topic that I don't feel has been adequately addressed for many reasons. But here, in the pages of this book, I want to offer truth to you wrapped in love, so that we can come out of denial, so that we can become more aware, so that we can create a new pattern of parenting and "training up" between ourselves and our sons. Maybe you can relate to the following. I was a mother who…….

- loved her son more than anything and anyone else (even myself),
- idolized her son,
- gave her son anything he wanted,
- didn't know how to say No to her son,
- treated her son as her possession,
- raised her son to fill her love void,
- ignored signs that her son was in trouble,
- didn't know her own power,
- suffered from low self-esteem and a lack of self-love,
- didn't know how to love, and
- *loved her son to death*

Mothers, we are loving our sons to death! Mothers we have over-loved our sons, maybe even "s-mothered" our sons and not raised them. Mothers, I've heard us call our sons little man, our best friend, my king, even my significant other. Mothers, I've heard us speak to our sons and about our sons as if they were our boyfriends, our husbands, or our possessions. In essence, mothers have made their sons into their little men, their king, their best friends, their "mini me's," their reason for living, their answer, their one and only, their everything - all roles a son cannot and should not be expected to fulfill. This creates high expectations a son can never live up to or fulfill.

Mothers it is time for us to wake up and rise up as parents, to heal our own wounds, to face the truth, to walk in our power as mothers, and take back our sons.

As mothers, we have been given the assignment to give life and "train them up," and instead we have been disempowering them, often unintentionally, and crushing their spirits instead. Too often, we've unconsciously been using our sons to try to get what we yearned for from our fathers, what we feel our boyfriends or baby's Daddy took from us, and our husbands aren't giving us.

We have been misplacing the burden on our sons to give to us the love we desired from certain adult men in our lives, to be the male who wouldn't abandon us, to be the male who would love us, to be the male who would give us affection, to be the male who would bring meaning to our life.

The truth is that we thought we were protecting them, that we were providing them with the love and material possessions that we didn't get as a child. We thought that if we loved them enough they would heal our broken hearts. We thought that by putting all of our efforts and energy into being the most loving and understanding mother, that our sons would become great men. We thought that we were showing them the love we longed for, that we were giving them a voice that we didn't have, that we were raising them to not be like their fathers nor our fathers.

Mothers, we had great intentions, we did our best, but, we are loving our sons to death!

I say, with compassion, enough is enough! Let's take back our power as women, as mothers, as leaders, as healers. Let's stop passing the blame and take full responsibility for our part in parenting our sons.

Let's vow to raise our sons to be strong, educated, respectful men with high self-esteem and self-confidence. Let's recognize our sons as gifts and not property. Let's take back our sons whether we gave birth to them or not. Let's vow to stand in our rightful place as mothers, stop trying to be their friends and do the inner work that is needed in to heal our brokenness, our disappointment, our own feelings of abandonment and rejection, and our own rage.

Mothers, I am not by *any* means absolving fathers from their responsibility to love and raise their sons. Our sons desperately need their fathers to love them as well as the presence and support of other positive male role models to demonstrate and teach them how to be a man. We need this now more than ever, I am sharing from my perspective and my experience coaching, speaking to, and working with *many* mothers of sons, many of who are raising them alone. For us to save our sons we also need the healthy participation of fathers, too, but this book is about us and for us as mothers.

Mothers, I love you, I stand with you!
Mothers, we can heal ourselves so that we can heal our sons!
Mothers, we can lead the revolution to save our sons!
This book is not about blame, though it is about telling the truth. This book is not about condemnation, though it is about "owning" our power and ability as mothers to profoundly shape and influence the identity, self-esteem and self-concept of our sons. I am here and this book is here to be your guide, to be your support, and to lead you down the path of healing, restoration, and empowerment, as a mother and especially as the mother of a son/sons.

Are you with me??

To Mothers Raising Sons

Author's Note

This book includes my personal experience of raising a black son and the many painful but powerful lessons learned. Unbeknownst to me, I was unconsciously trying to create my son to ***my*** "perfect man." As a young mother, I chose to raise my son without his biological father because of my experience growing up without my father and not seeing many of my friend's fathers in the home. I believed a father wasn't necessary to raise a child. I didn't realize it at the time, but I had low personal self-esteem and had a very damaged self-concept. I experienced many sleepless nights and heartbreak from men who I thought loved me.

In this book, I will take you along the tumultuous ride of attempting to raise a healthy young Black man when in fact I was emotionally unhealthy myself. Raised by a single mother, I was conditioned to believe that I didn't need a man or anyone for that matter, to help me. I didn't realize that I was parenting from a "flawed model," where I was determined to shower him with my version of love, one that would compensate for the love I didn't receive as a child, to give him what I believed I didn't have materially, and to allow him to express himself since I felt stifled as a child.

I share from my experience of coaching and mentoring mothers of black sons as well as from my own lived experience. I have found a pattern among mothers of essentially, "loving our sons to death." By this I mean using the explanation of "I love him" as a default for not allowing him to learn from his mistakes, not holding him accountable for his decisions and choices, for choosing to reward bad behavior, by continuing to shower him with gifts, and continually coming to his defense when he gets himself in trouble. I found that this way of relating to our sons is widespread and nearly an epidemic, even with mothers who had the fathers as partners or husbands present. You might think that married mothers and mothers who have support from their son's fathers would be exempt from this dynamic. My research shows that this is not so. In my situation, I was married and my husband (step-father to my son) was active in my son's life. However, I sabotaged him at every turn because he was "my son" and I was in control. I've noticed that this "control" dynamic exists especially with mothers who suffer from low self-esteem, lack self-confidence, and they don't even realize it. I didn't.

This dynamic of loving our sons to death is exasperated when a mother is raising her son without the father's presence and active participation. The son can then become her "Replacement Man." The mother unconsciously tries to make her son "the man of her dreams." As a result, she can unconsciously elevate her son to filling the roles in her life as a boyfriend, husband or father, the son then becomes responsible for the mother's heart or her fulfilling her emotional needs in exchange for theirs. The mother becomes dependent on her son to make her feel loved, needed, valued and wanted which causes her to "s-mother" her son. This cripples the son's ability to develop emotional maturity and wisely manage his emotions.

I use real life mother/son relationship scenarios throughout the book to help the reader understand the mother/son relationship dynamic *up close* and in vivid detail. In the coaching sessions I have with mothers, I have witnessed some amazing changes once mothers have started to acknowledge these dynamics, begin their own healing, and start to engage very differently with their sons. I've witnessed sons return home after being a run-away for months, sons changing their negative behavior at home and school; mothers setting healthy boundaries and no longer allowing their sons to manipulate them, mothers accepting their sons for who they are versus trying to turn them into who they need them to be and who they want them to be, and the communication between the two of them being reestablished or improved.

The Day My Life Changed

On March 29, 2013, my beloved son K'Breyan Clark was murdered at the age of 19. He was my only child. As you can imagine, I was devastated. This wasn't the end that I had worked for, prayed for and desired for my son. It was this devastating event that awakened me, and after a bout with depression, gave me the strength and the sense of urgency to help other mothers do their inner work. This equips them to love from a healthy place and in turn, to positively impact the emotional well-being and self-concept of their sons.

How to Get the Most from This Book

The message I share, as tough as it may be to hear and accept, comes from a deeply loving place. It comes from a place of compassion for the mother's journey, and an understanding of how powerful and pivotal a mother is in her son's life. Ultimately, this book is about understanding your power as a woman and as a mother to positively influence the life of your son/sons. The intent is to cause mothers to make the decision to do the necessary self-work required to heal, to help them begin their healing, and to then be able to go forward parenting very differently, or helping other mothers parent differently.

There is a startling rise in the amount of young black men being killed. Homicide is the second leading cause of death for young people, ages 15 – 24 years old. In fact, in 2010, an average of 13 mothers a day received a call that their son had been shot and killed. It is critically imperative that mothers raising black sons understand how the degree of their own emotional health critically impacts the development, identity, communication, and coping skills of their sons. We are in a state of emergency!

I urge you to read the words I've written in these pages without judgment, without attaching right or wrong, without feeling attacked, and without being defensive. Instead, I invite you to open your heart to receive truth. This truth can transform you, your son, and your relationship with him.

I am fully aware that you may be operating within paradigms you acquired from the parenting you personally received or witnessed. The thought of going against these traditions may even bring up some resistance. You might have even vowed *not* to perpetuate an aspect of parenting that one or both of your parents may have modeled, that did not work for you, or that you hated. Then you look up, and you're perpetuating the exact things that you hated when you were being parented. Or sometimes, we swing the pendulum too far in the opposite direction because we want to be sure we *don't* do what our parents did. However, this can create an imbalance, but in the opposite direction.

My advice to you is to allow your desire to raise a healthy son to be greater than the fear of change or of the unknown. Your son's very life depends on your willingness to seek out, face, and tell the truth, first, to yourself.

How this Book is Organized

This book is organized in three parts. Part I includes Chapters 1-3 which tells the story of how I raised my son during his early years. These chapters explain what beliefs and behaviors influenced the way I raised my son and how my lack of self-esteem affected how I raised him. Part II includes Chapter 4-7 which chronicle my son's rebellion, my guilt, my shame and our restoration. These chapters will take you on the ride of a confused mother doing the best she knew how do to, a rebellious teenager, and also wonderful lessons of grace. Part III includes Chapters 8-10 which take you on a journey of loss, healing and triumph. These chapters will break your heart, get your attention, help you turn pain into a greater purpose and give you hope. After each chapter, there are exercises to help you reflect on and confront experiences that formed the way you parent, both consciously or unconsciously. My personal story and the stories of other mothers are meant to help you recognize the connection between your childhood experiences and the unhealthy beliefs that affect how you train up your son. These realizations are meant to give you a new awareness of where some of your parenting behaviors stem from, the need to heal emotionally and the power you have as a mother to raise a healthy son.

When mothers aren't healed and whole, it affects the psyche, emotional, mental, and even spiritual development of our sons. It affects entire generations. I shed light on the unintended behavioral consequences in their sons when mothers aren't whole.

I address the unique connection with mothers and their male children. Research shows that the love of a mother can and does actually make boys stronger, emotionally, and psychologically, however, if the mother is emotionally unhealthy, her expression of love can have an adverse effect on how a son recognizes and expresses his own feelings.

With a growing epidemic of murders of black males and high incarceration rates, women are left to raise their sons, many of them alone. As a result women are assuming a role that they weren't equipped to fulfill and they can fall into what comes natural to them as a woman- to love and nurture. However, in the name of loving them, it's been without disciplining them effectively, without providing clear and appropriate consequences, without empowering them to be capable, responsible, and without giving them healthy and reasonable challenges that would grow them, stretch them and build their inner resilience. Instead, in the name of loving them, we coddled them, we spoiled them, over-protected them, allowed them to do whatever they wanted, have whatever they wanted, and get away with bad behavior. We weren't firm with our "No's," didn't require them to respect themselves or others, didn't require them to earn their way, or take responsibility for their actions.

Unintentionally, we end up damaging, stifling or handicapping our sons' development. The truth is that many of us don't know how to actually "train up" a son so that he receives what develops and strengthens the Black male character and spirit. I know that I sure didn't. Maybe we didn't know how to render effective discipline, accountability and teach them responsibility in a way that it clicked for them. Instead we often defended or justified poor or lazy behavior.

Lastly I will discuss the correlation between women who are love-frustrated, have a history of disappointing or failed love relationships with adult men, or have a "Daddy-yearning" can subconsciously seek to have their "inner holes" filled by their sons.

My desire is that you will be able to see yourself or someone you know in these pages and, most importantly, that you will take immediate action so that a mother can be healed, a Black son is saved, and a mother is spared from burying her child.

Chapter 1

The Frankenstein Syndrome

Creating the Perfect Man

I was six months pregnant before I got excited about being a mother. I lived in Houston at the time living with a group of women who were all attending Texas Southern University (TSU). I had attended TSU two years prior and, because of financial reasons, had to drop out in Feb 1989. I moved back to Seattle, WA with the intention to save money, return to Houston to live, and eventually go back to TSU. In 1991 I moved to Houston, got a job and lived between my apartment and the apartment of some girlfriends who attended TSU. Life in Houston was filled with partying and more partying. In August of 1992 after thinking I was experiencing the longest hangover ever, my supervisor convinced me to take a pregnancy test. I found out I was pregnant. To say I was surprised is an understatement. Because of all the unprotected sex I had in a previous relationship, with not even one pregnancy scare, I had convinced myself I was unable to conceive. The only guy I'd loved wasn't really my boyfriend. We had what you would call a "booty call" type of relationship. I was the "side chick."

At the time I got pregnant, I had just turned 23, and had been promoted to a full-time Office Manager position at the South Central YMCA. I'd felt like my life in Houston was finally starting to shape up like I had hoped. And certainly a baby wasn't part of my plan. I was living the life of a college student having booty calls with someone I barely knew. *A baby surely didn't fit into this picture.*

I had planned to abort the pregnancy and even scheduled two appointments to do so. The first time while in Houston and then I had to reschedule to have it done in Seattle. When I arrived at the clinic in Houston, the sidewalk in front of the clinic was lined with protestors. I dared not cross the protestor's line so I attempted to find another clinic. I soon discovered that all the abortion clinics in Houston were the scene of protests. So, I decided to have the abortion at a clinic back home in Seattle instead. I had the money in hand and was ready, but this time I was so ill I couldn't leave the house. The illness lasted the entire week I was home. Before I knew it, my time in Seattle had come to an end and I had to return to Houston without the abortion.

Not being able to have the abortion twice seemed to be a sign to me. I became convinced that I was meant to have this baby. I was scared to tell Dallas, the man with whom I had the "booty call" relationship with that I was pregnant and keeping the baby. I remember the very day I conceived. He asked me if I wanted him to use protection and I said No. To this day, I'm not sure why I said No, but in that moment I gave him permission not to use a condom. That day would be our last sexual encounter. When I was five months pregnant, I decided to move back to Seattle. The thought of telling Dallas I was pregnant, that I was keeping "it" and that I was moving back to Seattle, terrified me. To my surprise, he believed the baby was his when I told him, and he showed a glimmer of excitement - all which made me feel like I'd made the right decision.

Here I was, on the plane heading home to Seattle, five months pregnant, with no job, no money, and moving back in with my mother. I became overwhelmed with sadness. This scenario did not fit the plan I had for myself, at all. I cried, missing Dallas though we only had a sexual relationship. I was plagued with questions. My stomach was in knots. *Was I making the right decision? Should I have stayed?* In Houston, I had a job with benefits, an apartment and lots of support. "It must be the hormones," I thought to myself. There was no other good reason why, all of a sudden, I felt regret. While midway through the airplane flight back to Seattle, I wiped away my tears and told myself, *"You got this. You can do this. You will not become a single mom statistic."* This was the start of my stance to prove to his father that I didn't need him or his help to raise this child. Not that this was a conversation we had, but it was based in my belief and conditioning from my upbringing that I didn't need a man. I wanted him to know his participation and presence was optional. I also wanted to prove to my mother that I would raise this child by myself, and do a damn good job at it. I had watched her raise my sister's son and heard her judgment and opinion about it often, so I was determined not to follow my sister's footsteps.

Once home with my mother I started fantasizing about my unborn child. If it's a boy, his name would be different so he'd stand out from the other boys. Everyone would know him, of course, he would be popular, cute, smart, funny, athletic, and have a little swag. He would graduate from college and have a successful life like the men on TV. He would have the same initials as me and his dad - KC. That's what they'd called me in college.

I remembered this fine guy in college named KayBee and every girl on campus loved to say his name. I thought to myself, his nickname will be KB, so that whatever name I come up with would be sure to have those initials. I was convinced that this baby would make me whole, that he was a gift from God to give me all the love I didn't feel that I got as a child.

While he was in my womb, I began creating a life in my mind, based on my unfulfilled desire to be loved by my father as a little girl. My father lived out of state and I didn't see him much. We spent a couple of summers with him in California and I cherished this time with him. I loved my father and I wanted him to rescue me from the life I had in Seattle. In my mind, he was rich, and living with him would give me the love and material things I constantly dreamt about and wished for growing up. This yearning for attention and affection I longed for from my father and mother was combined with my thwarted desire to be loved and accepted by the man I was head over heels for in high school. I vowed to myself that I would raise my son so differently from how I was raised. My mother, a MSW, worked hard to keep a roof over our heads and as a result I didn't see her much. And when I did, she seemed angry that she was raising five children on her own. I watched her struggle to pay bills and to keep food in the house. She came home from work depleted and retreated to her room to read one of the many books that lined the bookshelves in our home. Often, I was afraid to talk to her, I feared her rejection, but as much as I feared her, I desired her affection and her presence. I perceived I was a bother to her, a reminder that her marriage to my father failed. I felt like I was a burden. As a child, I always wanted more, more love, more affection, more affirmation, and more time with those I loved.

In my mind, my son would be the answer to my dreams of having it all - a man, family, and love. It didn't seem that my father and mother really loved me, but my son surely would love me. We would be the family I dreamed of as a child. We would spend a lot of time together; we would have a nice home, nice clothes and food, lots of it, and he could eat anything he wanted, when he wanted. This was because growing up we didn't get to eat what we wanted, my mom always seemed to be on a diet, so our food was limited to what she could eat like, boiled eggs, cottage cheese and tuna. It was a far cry from the types of things the other kids brought to school in their lunches. Because my parents were divorced we had visitation with our dad, but he was a vegetarian and diabetic, so we didn't get to eat meat or sugar while with him. This was on top of the fact that my mom was raising five kids on a tight budget. So, my goal was to make sure *my* child would have it all, would never want for anything, and would never feel like he was a burden.

I had already planned his entire life out in my head. This is the point where I began creating the "perfect" man in my mind. I prayed earnestly that he would be handsome. His dad had a peculiar nose and I sure didn't want him to inherit that! I thought hard about how I would dress him, how he would look. As it turns out, I wanted him to look like the men I desired but was never able to attract. He was going to treat me like a queen, take care of me when I got older, *not* be like the men I'd dated, and most importantly, *not* turn out like the men in my family. He was going to be the one that broke the cycle of men who mistreated women and who sold and did drugs. All of what I had been exposed to as a child and a young girl in the dating scene scarred me. As a young girl I was exposed to men who used women for sex and money, who didn't commit to a relationship and who slept around. I watched the women in my life put up with this and watched the men in my life perpetuate it. When I began dating I seemed to attract the same type of men and found myself being okay with being used. I accepted this as my destiny when it came to men. Because of these experiences, I had created a perfect role for my son in my fantasies, his fate was already sealed at least in my mind. I was going to do everything in my power to make it all come true.

As a young mother who was wounded emotionally I created a life for my unborn child based on my need for love- my unhealthy understanding of the meaning of love. I saw my child as the answer to my constant prayer for real love and placed undue responsibility on him to fulfill my need for an emotional savior. What I didn't know at the time, was that the fantasy of a young mother who lacked self-love would hold such dire consequences in both me and my son's life.

Coddling our Sons

As KB grew so did his personality, popularity, good looks and talent on the basketball court. I was so proud of my son - he was turning out *just* the way I had planned it. Looking back however, there were many signs that my son's emotional health was in trouble – there were calls from the school, him bragging to his friends, his constant desire for new clothes, and toys, his anger when disciplined by his stepfather, and his volatile behavior on the basketball court. At the time, I chose to see these as normal young boy behaviors. This was in spite of the many warnings from those around me that he had anger issues, was spoiled, was using me, and was out of control.

As I look back on this period of his upbringing, I can now admit that I coddled him. I allowed him to argue with me and others without consequence. I continued to spoil him despite the many calls from school and I shielded him from taking responsibility for his behavior. In my mind, he was "my baby." I immediately stood up for him and "protected" him by defending him to school disciplinarians, no matter what his part was in the incident. To make matters worse, I constantly undermined his stepfather's authority by:

- Lifting his restrictions or not enforcing them,
- Voicing my disagreement with his step-father's decisions in front of KB,
- Altering his restrictions,
- Giving my husband the silent treatment when I disagreed with his discipline of KB, or
- Hiding KB's behavior from him.

I did all of this at the risk of causing a strain in the relationship with my husband, which it did. I allowed my son to lay with me in the bed until he was fourteen, at the dismay of my husband. This should have been our sacred space as husband and wife, but I would argue, "He's my baby." These words would come back to haunt me in KB's later teenage years. I babied him his entire life, even after he was a legal adult.

Idolizing our Sons

Though it's hard to admit, I idolized my son by putting his wants before my own and even before my marriage. Even if it meant bills went unpaid so that I could buy him expensive clothes and the latest shoes. I wanted him to have what I didn't have. I wanted him to look and play the part of perfection. After all, he was my biggest success. He was my pride and joy. If he looked good, I felt good. I bragged about his accomplishments, his good looks and his talent on the basketball court. All of this made me feel special. He was the superstar and I felt "lucky" to be his mother. I basked in the attention he received, and contributed even more to this by coddling him. Vicariously, he gave me the popularity I never had. I *loved* being asked if I was KB's mom. Yes, I was living vicariously through him because in my own personal life, I didn't feel there was enough success, accomplishments or achievements to feel pride nor joy about.

Why? Because my self-esteem had all kinds of holes in it and my self-confidence was inexistent.

The truth is that the relationship with my son had mirrored the relationship I had with a man for 10 years – with someone that was always someone else's boyfriend. I was the side chick for 10 years. I showered him with gifts, my love, turned a blind eye to his bad behavior, and believed that if I continued to buy him nice things and be there whenever he needed me, that somehow, he would eventually love me and would be the man I longed for. In some way, I believed that the reason he couldn't commit to me was because of me and not him, that I was the one who needed to make adjustments, not him. I didn't understand that how I navigated this relationship, suppressed my emotions and feelings to keep the relationship alive, would have a direct impact on how I raised my son and how he would handle his own emotions.

In both relationships, as the 10-year side chick and with my son, I thought that by giving them whatever they wanted, whether it was money, clothes, shoes or time with me, this was a guarantee that they would love me back in return. I also believed that if I didn't give them what they wanted, they would reject me and not give me the love I desired. I had love and material possessions inextricably linked. I was trying to *buy* love.

I-Don't-Need-a-Man Attitude

I was a master at undermining my husband's discipline. We could never agree on what the appropriate punishment would be for KB. His consequences were always too strict for me. This is where I took the opportunity to assert control because, after all, KB was "my son." And what my husband had to say really didn't matter. I always had the final say. I knew how to yell loud, threaten and bully him, all enough to guarantee I got my way. It didn't take long for KB to see who was in charge, and boy did he know how to play this to his advantage. I hate to admit this now. KB would give me the silent treatment and cast his eyes at me whenever he overheard me telling Raymond he had gotten in trouble at school. He would wait until we were alone and say, "Why did you tell him?" He made feel like I was betraying him whenever I involved Raymond in disciplining him. When I asked KB what was wrong with him, he always replied, "You!" This made feel me terrible and responsible for his happiness and the more he said it, the more I let him get away with his bad behavior. Because of the love we had for one another I thought I could influence and control his behavior, quickly this proved not to be the truth.

My truth was that I learned how to be overly independent watching my mom raise five children by herself. I believed that I could raise my child on my own. In fact, this was my thought when I packed my bags and left Houston for Seattle. I had the attitude that I was an independent woman and I don't need a man to help me raise *my* child. This belief manifested in how I undermined my husband's discipline at every turn. This thinking was my justification for my choice not to include KB's biological father in my decision to leave Houston and move back to Seattle to raise our child. I didn't even consider his opinion, and frankly, I didn't give a damn about his opinion. I operated under the belief that I would be a single mother and a damn good one at that.

I soon learned how this behavior would contribute to the way my son interacted with his stepfather. Their relationship was filled with arguments, silent treatments, and a mild disdain for one another. It was as if I was living with a feuding husband and my boyfriend.

I constantly was in the middle of their arguments, forced to take sides, and always trying to explain the actions of the other. KB thought I loved his stepfather more than I loved him and said it often. He was jealous of him. But little did he know that my husband was jealous of him, too. KB didn't understand the love we had for each other as husband and wife, couldn't be compared. I always told KB that because he was my son, our relationship would last forever and that me and his stepfathers relationship wasn't an ironclad guarantee and could end as a result of death or divorce. In retrospect, this gave KB the upper hand in his mind.

In my mind, the fact that he wanted to "hog me all to himself," got twisted and used to validate that I was loved, special, and needed. All the things I yearned for an adult man to feel towards me seemed to be coming from my son. Because my son loved me like this, I felt like I had succeeded at the goal of ensuring he would never leave me like the other men had done in my past, including my father.

The Vicious Cycle

As a daughter of a mother who experienced a deficit in her self-love, self-esteem, and self-confidence. I learned how to be overly-independent, overly self-sufficient, and believing that you couldn't rely on others, only yourself. From my perspective my mother wasn't successful with men. Her divorce from my father was painful and I watched her argue with him every time he was around. I saw her cry way too many times over men who hurt her and abandoned her. I witnessed men disrespect her, including the men in her family. As a child my grandfather would visit us often and then one day it ended. I didn't know why but I knew he had done something that hurt her profusely. My grandmother was what you call "old school" and seemed calloused and uncaring. She and my mom didn't have the greatest of relationships and I often overheard my grandmother say mean things about my mom, her parenting, and her relationships with men. My mom always had women over the house whom she counseled, who I thought were her friends. I witnessed them go from loving relationships to nothing. I wondered where all these women went and why they didn't come to visit my mom anymore. It seemed that my mom couldn't keep a man nor women friends. I look back as an adult and have a better understanding of how the unhealed hurts from her childhood and adulthood had an impact on the way she loved us, and all the pain she endured while trying to raise five children on her own.

My mom was harder on my two older sisters than she was on my brother. He was able to stay out later and do less chores when compared to my sisters. In my mind, she seemed to love him more than any of us. Even though I know this isn't true, as a child, it appeared that way to me. And because my mom couldn't give me the affection, adoration, affirmation, and acknowledgement I needed and desired as a child. I used my accomplishments, brains and accumulation of nice things to compensate and fill those voids.

I find this to be true with the mothers I've coached. If they were raised by a mother who struggled with self-love they, like myself, mothered their sons in a way that resulted in their sons not learning responsibility, being overly-dependent upon women, and expecting women to provide for them. This is because their mothers, for many reasons, weren't able to instill what they themselves didn't have - a high level of self-esteem and self-worth. This generational dynamic then resulted in us, the daughters of these mothers, seeking validation from men, including their sons. Some, on the other hand, parented just like their own mothers, even if they despised their own upbringing, and despite their desire to parent differently.

In my work with mothers, and in healing from my own mothering journey, I've found the surprising and profound correlation between a mother's low self-esteem and self-love; her internal beliefs, thoughts and behaviors; how they manifest in her behavior towards her son, and how they manifest in her son's self—concept, and behavior towards himself and others.

The following chart illustrates these correlations.

Mother's internal beliefs, thoughts, and behaviors	How it Manifests in Son's Thoughts and Behavior
I am not lovable. I have to work for love or I have to prove that I'm loveable.	• Become spoiled and conditioned to think they are "entitled" and should get whatever they want. They can become a user of women
I need to be liked/people pleaser.	• Think others owe them • Displays anger when told No • Will do whatever is necessary to get what he wants • Will use women
Outer appearance must be impeccable/ masks hurt and low self-image.	• Becomes addicted to nice things and overly defined by material things • Hides true feelings • Becomes superficial
A man completes me.	• Controls mother with threats • Manipulates her to get his way
Undermines disciplinary action/ defends his bad behavior.	• Doesn't accept responsibility for his bad behavior • Doesn't recognize bad behavior as unacceptable

	- Doesn't take feedback well
	- Doesn't respect the disciplinarian
Screams and yells at him when he makes a mistake.	- Lies - Hides mistakes - Doesn't confide in mother - Keeps secrets - Becomes deceptive
Doesn't spend a lot of time with him.	- Doesn't feel secure within himself - Exhibits fear - Susceptible to gangs (desiring belonging and a family) - Drug and/or substance use
Pushes him into sport/schools/career you desire for him.	- Rebels - Doesn't express his creativity - Leads a double life; one in front of his parents and a secret one with friends
Talk disparagingly about his father/men.	- Loses respect for his father and other men - Has difficulty with male authority figures - Develops self-hate

	· Becomes overly effeminate · Doesn't receive feedback well
Doesn't admit or own up to mistakes/redirects when confronted.	· Mirrors the behavior · Not able to admit when wrong · Challenges with seeing another perspective

Reflection

Your story may not be the same as mine and you may have not had the same experiences I had growing up. However, I challenge you to reflect on how you were raised and how it caused you to set out to parent or not to parent, the way your mother and/or father did. What I've since learned is that as a child, my perceptions were based on my limited understanding and perspective, and not absolute truth. However, for many years, these perceptions became my truth, and from them I formed beliefs that I was unwanted, unlovable and that I didn't matter. It was these beliefs that I parented from – a place of "unhealedness," and I wanted to ensure my son never felt the way I did as a child. These beliefs birthed behaviors that were counterproductive to raising an emotionally healthy son.

The good news is that if you recognize any personal thoughts or behaviors in this chapter, you have the power to change your beliefs and heal from your past wounds. It's not too late!

Reflection Questions:

1. What thoughts/behaviors do you recognize within yourself?
2. What thoughts/behaviors do you recognize manifesting in your son?
3. What thoughts/behaviors from the previous chart do you need to examine/address?
4. What correlations do you notice?
5. How did your own upbringing affect your parenting decisions?

Chapter 2

Working for the Love of our Sons

I rarely said, No to KB and when I did, I almost always would bend the rules or eventually say Yes. There was nothing that I wouldn't do for him and nothing I wouldn't give him. I did this, to the disappointment of my husband and with ridicule from my friends and family. Sure, I heard the rumors, the gossip, and even was counseled by those older and wiser than me. None of this mattered, nor did it penetrate, because in my mind, only *I* knew what was best for *my* son, *so I thought*. As far as I was concerned, this was *my* business and I wanted others out of it. Frankly, at the time, I didn't see what the problem was anyway. I didn't realize how many blind spots I had. I didn't realize that my wounds and inner voids were determining how I parented, not me.

When it came to KB, I had so many blind spots. I can admit to being in denial as his behavior worsened, but in the beginning, I just didn't see an issue with his behavior. Because of the relationship we had, and my mindset at the time, I believed I could "make" him act right if I said or did the right thing. My inability to see the full extent of the problem was coupled with my intent to protect and insulate him from what could potentially equate to him being hurt, embarrassed, or mistreated. As a child I was often made to feel embarrassed because we didn't have the food, money, and family structure that my friends had. My twin sister and I seemed to be the butt of many jokes because we were "poor." Our neighbors dressed us and fed us, but not without the constant "whispers" about their feelings about our mother's absence. I grew to believe the only way I could be liked is if it I had money and material things. So I set out to protect my son from the potential of negative opinions and ridicule from others, like I had experienced. I *ensured* that he had nice things and I came to his defense when I felt he was being attacked. However, in doing this he was ill-equipped to manage rejection and remain confident in himself no matter what others thought of him. I was quick to always defend him and stand up for "my baby" especially when men told me that I needed to toughen up my discipline on him and to stop treating him like a baby. By protecting him, I became his "savior," and I taught him that I would always bail him out of any situation in which he found himself. As a result he didn't adequately develop the ability to resolve conflicts, work through his emotions, or "own" his mistakes. Unknowingly, I had handicapped him.

Because my own self-esteem was low and I was operating from an unhealed place, in my mind I felt they were criticizing what was my life saver. Though they were right, at the time, I misinterpreted their advice and care as criticism and judgment. I vehemently asserted that I was a good parent and knew what was best for my son, leaving no room for argument or to even "hear" what others were trying to tell me. No matter what they said, what I *heard* was, "You are a bad mother," and responded as such, rendering my friends and family silent, as they were forced to stand by and silently watch everything unfold.

As you examine your own parenting, where have you been guilty of protecting your son from experiencing and working through hurt, embarrassment or mistreatment in a healthy way?

I've since witnessed this same dynamic play out with mothers and their sons countless times, especially when they are being given feedback by their son's father, their husband/boyfriend or any other male figure. Men can clearly see and know how the lack of discipline will manifest in the son's behavior, if left unchecked, and they can attempt to talk with the mother. However, she tends to reject their advice and asserts that she knows what's best for her son. I believe women as the nurturers often continue to see their son as their baby and don't always adapt their parenting style to reflect the current age and maturity of their growing son. This is why it is so important for there to be a positive, strong male presence in a young boy's life.

I vowed that any child of mine wouldn't grow up having to ask for anything. I wanted my son to have the material things I didn't have and especially the more expensive clothes and shoes I didn't get because we couldn't afford them when I was growing up. I wanted him to have the latest clothes, shoes and haircuts. So when he asked for something, I said Yes. I remember him asking me for $1500 to buy a car (and mind you, he didn't even have a license.) Sure, I knew this was a ridiculous request, but how could I say No? This was one of the first times I actually hesitated and took inventory of my behavior and I decided to go against my normal routine, and talk it over with someone else.

At the time, KB was nineteen years old and I was going to a counselor. We discussed my dilemma about not knowing how to say No to my son. She asked me one question that would eventually set me free. "What do you think would happen if you said No?" I was immediately taken aback, "What would happen?" I thought. Before I knew it, I had blurted out the answer, "He wouldn't love me." I was shocked at my response. In my twisted inner belief system, I believed that if I didn't say yes to my son he wouldn't love me anymore, would withdraw his love from me, and might even abandon me. I chalked this up to meaning: I would feel lonely, rejected, and it would mean that I had failed as a mother, *and* as a person. This kind of perceived "double failure" was my greatest nightmare.

Think back to a time when, against your better judgment, you gave your son something extravagant, said Yes,

or rewarded him when he didn't deserve it. **What was your greatest fear if you said No?**

Working for His Love

I didn't realize it at the time, but what I had been doing for so many years was working for my son's love. I believed that his love for me was conditional – dependent upon what I gave him, what I did for him, and what I allowed him to do. This belief spilled over into *all* my relationships, especially my friendships. I constantly suppressed my true feelings because I felt that if I disagreed with a friend, they would reject me. I prided myself in being the one they could confide in and who would never challenge them, even when they were wrong. My low self-esteem led me to suppress my voice and accept poor treatment by others. I believed that people loved me because of what I gave them and what I did for them, this included my son. This stemmed from my lack of self-love and low self-esteem.

As a child I rationalized in my young mind that the reason why I only saw my father some summers and talked to him only on my birthday and Christmas was because he didn't love me. I rationalized that the reason my mother didn't spend the time with me that I wanted was because there was something inherently wrong with me. Otherwise, why wouldn't she consider me more important in her life?

This started me down a long path of trying to *prove* to others, men especially, that I was lovable. The form this proving took was giving them whatever they asked for and not holding them responsible for their bad behavior towards me. While in college I sent $500 of my financial aid award to the guy whom I was the "side chick," so he could buy a car - even though he was dating someone else. Even after we argued because I brought up the other women in his life, I would use promises of gifts, money and sex to lure him to my house.

I even did this with God. I believed that if I studied the Bible enough, memorized enough Bible verses, prayed constantly, always tried to be perfect, and donated hours of my time in service to my church, that I would prove to God that I was lovable, and then He would love me. I believed that I could *earn* God's love. I found myself working for everyone's love.

I even compromised relationships with those closest to me to please my son. Instead of loving our sons by teaching them independence, we are teaching our sons to become overly dependent on us. Unfortunately this type of "s-mothering" has an adverse effect. It can create a growing rage within a son and also cause him to desire to break free when he gets older, in an effort to have some independence from his mother.

I find that when mothers work for the love of their sons, this behavior is often mirrored in their love relationships with men and in other relationships. It often manifests through showering men with gifts, attention, and sex, despite the man's lack of commitment, respect or love towards the woman. All the more reason why it is critically important that women fall in love with themselves *first*, so they can create healthy relationships with others.

Being Too Permissive

Because of my yearning to be loved and my belief that I had to work to earn others' love, I gave my son permission and access to all of me, with virtually no privacy for myself. This included even busting in my bedroom without knocking first, talking to me like I was one of his homies, and manipulating me to get his way. It wasn't a big deal for me when he entered my room without knocking, however it infuriated my husband.

In my mind, it was as a sign that my son loved me and wanted to be around me. I couldn't understand why my husband had such a problem with this.

When I was growing up, my mom's room was off limits to us. This was one thing I didn't want to model with my son. I didn't want him to experience the rejection I felt when I stood outside her door and knocked, waiting for a response and denied permission to enter. Why couldn't I come in? Why couldn't I know what she was doing inside? I wanted KB to feel welcomed and thus I gave him the permission to come in my room whenever he wanted. As I have continued to uncover what is at the *root* of my behavior with my son, I now realize that, often it led back to painful (unhealed) memories and experiences from my own childhood that I didn't want KB to have to experience. The way I saw to remedy this was to allow the pendulum to swing in the entirely opposite direction. Too often, going to the extreme in the opposite direction fostered negative behaviors in KB.

I had dreamed of having a relationship where we would jump on the bed, watch television together, laugh, and fall asleep, just as I had seen on TV. It seemed so intimate, so idyllic and that's what I wanted to create. My love for him was so deep. I wanted him to feel safe, to feel loved and to feel wanted didn't feel. I unknowingly was trying to turn my son into "my fantasy man."

Hell, I didn't even know what boundaries were so they didn't exist in my relationship with my son. I later learned that by not establishing boundaries and being too permissive, my son didn't learn how to respect authority, or to hear No from someone else. It also interfered with my ability to set healthy limits for him. I acquiesced when he pressured me to change instead of requiring him to stick to any standards, limits or boundaries them. This translated into my son's struggle with accepting rejection well and his unrealistic, lofty expectations of me and the other women in his life. He believed women should give him whatever he wanted, when he wanted it.

For example, I often allowed him to spend the night over at a friend's house without checking to see if the home environment was appropriate. I assumed because they played on the same basketball team that this would be okay. I later found that at some of these homes, he was exposed to drug dealing, drug use, and violence. At some of the homes there wasn't adequate parental supervision and my son was allowed to roam the streets late into the night. It was these experiences that introduced him to the gang lifestyle early in his teens.

Where have you been too permissive with your son instead of establishing healthy boundaries?

Fear of Disappointment

One of my clients came to me because her son was behaving very badly. He was in and out of jail and violent. She was afraid for his life and knew she needed help. After our first conversation, it was apparent she hadn't set any boundaries for her son. She shared how she allowed him to come home at whatever time he pleased; she allowed him to smoke marijuana in her home; she constantly bailed him out of jail; she defended his bad behavior, and she allowed him to live with her as an adult, even after he would yell, scream and become uncontrollable. When I asked her why she allowed this behavior, she made excuse after excuse until she finally uncovered her truth. She loved him, but didn't know how to set boundaries while also loving him at the same time. She was afraid of disappointing him.

This fear of disappointment stemmed from her experience with her father. As a 9-year old child, she believed, she concluded that she was the reason that her father left never to return. This was the fear that was driving her inclination to do whatever it took to please her son. Because she was unhealed from the emotional wounds left behind by the "rejection" and "abandonment" of her father, she held a fear within her being that if she set boundaries with her son, he would reject her, abandon or leave her, as her father did - the man a young girl first loves.

Fear of Abandonment

As a young child I felt abandoned by my father. I couldn't understand why some of my friends' fathers were so active in their lives and mine wasn't. Even though my mom and dad weren't married, it still perplexed me. Why didn't my Dad live with us? Why wasn't my Dad involved in my life and my activities? This made me feel rejected and unlovable. To make it even more painful, I adored my dad. In my eyes, he was handsome, nice and rich - all which made it seem like I was robbed of the fairytale life I desired and saw on TV. I yearned to be a Daddy's girl. As sick and twisted as I now realize this thinking was, it was how I had things tee'd up in my head. It was this belief that kept me calling my son every day, telling him I loved him every day, wanting so badly to be his friend. I didn't want him to abandon me, too.

Then once I was in elementary school, I also felt abandoned by my mother when she began spending weekends with her boyfriend. She'd leave on Thursday night, not to return until Monday. This went on for many years. Even though my older siblings were home, I longed for her presence, despite, when she *was* at home, I still didn't get the attention I desired. To me, it seemed that I wasn't really wanted, valued and loved by *either* of my parents. This reinforced in my mind the perception that I was unworthy, unlovable, and unwanted.

In my household, we were taught that once you reach the age of eighteen, you leave home. All five of us not only knew this but were excited to leave home to create the life we desired. After we turned eighteen, a few of us came back home for short periods of time but for the most part, we left home and didn't turn back. So much so that we didn't spend a lot of time with our mother as adults either. Because of this dynamic that I have with my mom, I feared this would be the same kind of relationship I'd have with my son once he grew up. I wanted to be sure that me and my son were "tight," and not estranged.

Loving Too Much

I knew before my son was born that I would make sure he *knew* he was loved. When I was pregnant, I promised myself that my child would *never* have to question my love for him. Each time I saw KB, said goodbye to him or put him to sleep, I reminded him how much I loved him. My son extended the same courtesy to me, and I loved it. I loved hearing him say he loved me. What I found out much later was that my son defined love just as I had shown him, that love meant he could get his way and have whatever he wanted. So I obliged and loved him entirely too much for fear he would question my love. He would often use "love" against me and say, *"I thought you loved me"* or *"If you loved me, you would…"* He began to manipulate me because of our mutually warped understanding of love.

Loving too much or more accurately, using love to control, can lead to us making unhealthy decisions, in the name of love.

A Twisted Ideal of Love

In Christmas 2007, KB flew home to spend his winter break with us in Seattle. He had been in Texas for his freshman year in high school.

He spent most of those two weeks with his friends. It was like pulling teeth to get him to hang out with me. I remember sitting in the living room one morning, gazing out the window, and crying uncontrollably. My heart was broken. *"How could he do this to me after all I had done for him? Why wasn't he spending more time with me?!"* The internal emotions I was experiencing were as if my boyfriend was cheating on me or ignoring me - I felt helpless. I just knew that all those years of spoiling him and giving him whatever he wanted was a guarantee that he wouldn't leave me, would put me first, would show me affection, and make me feel loved by spending time with me. This was the first time I feared that he would abandon me, and I didn't like how it felt.

Many mothers I speak to operate under the same belief. They over-give, over-spend, over-allow, and over-defend in hopes that it guarantees they receive the male attention and love they desire in the form of him never abandoning her. This fear of abandonment is both a physical and an emotional abandonment. The unconscious hope and goal is that their son will fill the void they feel. The son then becomes their savior, the one who will rescue them, care for them and love them. This manifests in several ways, 1) mothers allowing their sons to essentially "get away with murder," 2) these sons having the misplaced emotional "burden" to fill the role of a missing husband, boyfriend or father, 3) to fill the fantasy of the Prince Charming or the "disappointment void" of the absent Prince Charming; and 4) we can attempt to make our sons fulfill this role through demands, manipulation and control. As a teenager, I overheard him many times telling girls he loved them. I knew he didn't, but was using these words to get what he wanted just as he had done with me for so long.

Referring to Him as "Your Baby"

Mothers will often see their sons as their "baby" even into adulthood. No matter how much he grows and ages we still see the baby, our baby. Because a baby, is dependent on its mother, mothers want to feel needed and for mothers of sons, by a male. This need for male love and acceptance causes us to s-mother or over love our son hoping we will get the same in return. When we refer to our son as our "baby" we are marking out territory as his mother, his first love, the queen, the first woman to have his heart.

We are essentially marking our territory so that other women are aware that our son will always love us more and will be most loyal to us. I believe this is one of the factors that results in mothers holding onto their sons well after they mature into adults, constantly bailing them out, babying them as teenager, adults, and by performing duties that should be done by their son. Sons that experience s-mothering like this usually end up in this manifesting in one of three ways: resenting women, abusing women or becoming overly effeminate. Sons that are overly effeminate are often exposed to conversations by their mother that belittle men or minimize the role of a father. This can be because of the mother's hurtful experiences with men and her desire to ensure her son doesn't become one of these men. This can cause self-hatred within the son making him fear his mother will eventually reject him as a man. Other manifestations of this affect include:

-the son not leaving home once he's an adult but "staying up under his mother,"

-the son becoming a dependent "Mama's Boy,"

-the mother constantly being displeased with their choice of girlfriends or wife, and/or

-the mother acting as if the son is "cheating" on her by being with another woman and she becomes intentionally divisive in their relationship out of a twisted form of jealousy.

One mother in particular shared with me how she couldn't stand her adult son's girlfriend. She believed the girlfriend was negatively influencing her son, and furthermore, it was the girlfriend's fault that her son moved out. She further stated that the girl was ugly, ghetto, and her son deserved better. When I suggested to her that she was jealous, she adamantly denied it. But eventually she came to her truth. In her mind, her son had chosen his girlfriend *over* her. I asked her if it was possible for her son to have a girlfriend while maintaining a relationship with her. *Why did the two need to be mutually exclusive?* I asked her. Because of her own fear of abandonment and her son filling the emotional role of boyfriend in her life for so many years, she perceived him moving in with a woman meant that their mother/son relationship was over. She also experienced similar types of internal emotions, *as if* she had actually been left by an adult male boyfriend or partner.

Reflection

Does of ANY of the scenarios in the reading above ring true for you? If so, where? What behavior do you notice – in the present or past? The good news is that even if you find yourself in the paragraphs above you can make small changes now to change your parenting by changing your beliefs. Here are some steps below to help change your behavior:

1. Acknowledge the behavior without judgment.
2. Recognize its root (where the behavior stems from).
3. Uncover the belief(s) created from the root.
4. Create a new healthy belief (s).
5. Create new behaviors based on the new belief(s).
6. Set new expectations with your son(s).
7. Seek an accountability partner to keep you accountable.

Reflection Questions

1. How have your past experiences with men, including your father spilled over to how you love and parent your son?
2. What is your greatest fear about your son?
3. What would happen if your greatest fear came true?

Giving Him What You Didn't Get

Even before I was pregnant, I knew I would give my child the physical and emotional things I didn't have as a child and what I felt I deserved. As a young child starting at age 9, I spent many days and nights asking God why I had the family I had and not the family of my neighbors and friends. I felt neglected and unloved by my mother and father. It wasn't until I was twenty-one that I first recall hearing the words *I love you* from my mother as she met me at the door with a hug, as I was leaving her house. I grew up feeling like I was a mistake, a hindrance, and unwanted. I never felt happy or joyous and I walked around angry and sad about my life at home. I never felt like a kid, my thoughts were filled with money worries, being hungry, and fear of disappointing my mom. I quietly feared I'd done something wrong or that she would explode if she came home and found that something wasn't in its rightful place or done to perfection. As a child I dreamt of what kind of mother I would be.

My mother was brilliant and you couldn't argue with her; you were guaranteed to lose. She was educated, read what seemed like a book a day, and was an avid truth teller. Her predictions always came true and somehow, she always knew why someone did what they did. Her words were eloquent, never colloquial and when I didn't understand a word she used, she steered to me a dictionary. People came from far and near for her advice and her ability to uncover truth was amazing, even though it was often met with dismay by those closest to her. She had the uncanny ability to see right through you. To me, it seemed that she always had to be right so I learned to suppress my opinions for fear of being scolded with her words, intense emotions or her verbal explosions. I learned from her how important it was to be smart and that this was her weapon and prized possession. While she couldn't give us material things, she gave us her brilliance.

As a single mother of five, she struggled to make ends meet, so having the latest clothes wasn't part of my reality. My clothes were often hand-me-downs from my older sisters or from neighbors. Food was sparse at times and we didn't have the permission to eat whatever we wanted. There were many days where all I ate was popcorn for dinner. I often dreamt of food and how, once I turned eighteen, my refrigerator would be filled with lots of ice cream and soda pop. A well-stocked kitchen made me feel rich and loved. This was what I vowed my son would have, along with having *new* clothes that were in style and from brand name stores. No hand-me-downs for my son!

I had grown conditioned to go without and not to ask for anything. I learned early on that asking didn't get you anything but a No and a lecture. This didn't stop me from hoping and wishing that birthdays and Christmases would be different each year, but I was disappointed time after time. Throughout my childhood, in our house, birthdays and Christmas were treated just like any other day. My child wouldn't experience this, I vowed. He would have *everything* he wanted and when he asked I would be able to say Yes. In my mind, this would confirm how much I loved him. He would also be able to express his wants and would have the freedom to talk to me about anything, something I didn't feel welcomed to do with my mother. My truth was that I equated food, clothes, and verbal self-expression with love. Because these were lacking for me, I vowed to "love" my son by giving him all of this and more. At the time, I didn't realize that this too was yet another form of overcompensating for where I had voids and unfulfilled desires.

This justification is common amongst the mothers I talk with. They believe their sons deserve what they didn't have, even at the risk of bills going unpaid. Each would tell me the same thing, and the story that served as the reason for their extravagant gifts and for ignoring their spoiled sons was surprisingly similar. As with my story, their ideal of showing love to their son was based on what they "did" as a mother and the thought that the more they "did" expressed how much they loved their son.

"Doing" a Mother is the idea that what we "do" or "don't do" is the metric that measures how good of a mother we are. Often, we "do" mothering based on what was or wasn't done for us as a child or in response to absent fathers or disappointed parents, so we've decided, "I can do this with or without you." And we go out to prove that "we can do this." The danger is that we will often grow to believe that DOing is required to love our son and when we can no longer DO we feel inadequate as a mother. And God forbid our son's start being ungrateful for what we are doing or begin to misbehave, we then are quick to say, "after all the things I've done for you, this is how you repay me?" We may also grow resentment towards him for not responding to our doing the way we envisioned. Our love has then become conditional and we are teaching him to love conditionally.

I was guilty of "doing" a mother and it wasn't until he began to rebel that I realized all I had done didn't exempt him from talking back, running away, getting into trouble, and not taking responsibility for his actions. All I had done seemed to backfire so I decided to do nothing else and started being his mother which meant saying no more than yes, not continually rescuing him and retiring my taxicab. The less I did the more he did!

I love having my grandson over the house. In preparation, I go to the store and buy all his favorites. One weekend he was scheduled to come over and I was tempted to cancel because I didn't have the money to buy his usual snacks and meals. As I thought about how I was going to break the news to his mother, God quickly reminded me that he wanted me, he wanted to be in my presence, it wasn't what I could do or buy for him, he wanted me, he wanted me to be his grandmother. That day, I was relieved of the need to do and I was free to just be.

DOing a Mother versus BEing a Mother

DOing	BEing
Spoiling him to replace your presence, to appease your guilt and despite his poor behavior.	Providing for his needs.
Using technology such as TV, computers, games, tablets and phones to keep him quiet or distracted.	Setting aside a designated time to connect with him.
Filling his day up with activities, parties and sleepovers so you can have some alone time.	Teaching him to honor your boundaries.
Not following through with discipline because it's too much work for you.	Disciplining him for poor behavior and following it through.
Buying him quick unhealthy meals that he loves because it's easier, more convenient for you or to make him happy.	Preparing meals with the food you have and including him whenever possible.
Driving him everywhere he wants to go.	Requiring him to use other resources to get him to and from where he wants to go.
Speaking for him, defending him to others and protecting him by sheltering him.	Teaching him how to make good choices and trusting he will make them when given the opportunity.

Even if you didn't do one more thing for your son he would love you. When I look back to my experience as a child, what I really wanted most from my parents was affection and attention. I believed the reason I didn't get the attention I so desired was because I had done something wrong. I set out to do everything right so they would come home, spend time with me, and love me. If you find yourself DOing more instead of just BEing, take small steps to break this cycle so that you and your son learn the valuable lesson that each of you are enough without having to do something to prove it. I challenge you to find ways to spend time with your son without spending money and without feeling the need to do something.

In the Name of Love

For years when questioned or challenged about my decisions regarding him I always responded with, "Because I love him." Not realizing that *what I was doing had nothing to do with the love I had for him but for the lack of love I had for myself.*

This is the same case that I found in a particular client. She was referred to me by a friend because her son's behavior had gotten increasingly worse and she feared for his safety as well as his possible arrest. When we met, she spent the first fifteen minutes explaining to me how sweet her son was and that he was smart and a good kid. Her love for him kept her from seeing and accepting the truth of what was really going on with him. He was a member of a gang, carried a gun and had been accused of murder. As she shared why she was concerned for his safety and her own, I listened and attempted to give her advice-which she rejected almost instantly. When I asked why she allowed this despicable behavior in her home, she said quickly, "Because I love him." She believed her loving him meant that she had to accept his bad behavior, tolerate disrespect, and subject herself to an unsafe environment. Interestingly, she accepted these same types of patterns of behavior from men in her romantic relationships. She believed that her "love" had the power to somehow change their behavior for the better. The more they acted up, the more she loved them, by giving in to their unreasonable demands, showering them with gifts, and constantly coming to their rescue. Little did she realize that she was mistaking love for dependency and expecting men to be like the "spackle" you use to fill holes in a wall, but in this case, she was treating them like "human spackle" that would fill the holes in her spirit.

This is a pattern with many of the mothers I've interviewed. They believe that the more they love their sons, the more love and affection they will get in return, as if love is the only thing required to raise a son. They believe their over-loving alone will ultimately redeem him and change his bad behavior.

I have noticed that many of us have a warped understanding of love believing that men, even our sons, complete us as women, thus placing an unhealthy expectation on our sons to make us whole and to fulfill our every need. I used love to explain why I spent my last dime on men, why I allowed them to treat me badly, and why I accepted being the other woman and "side chick" for 10 years when I really desired to be the "main" chick and "the" girlfriend. My confusion and misunderstanding of love spilled over to my relationship with my son and I found myself giving the same excuse when questioned why I didn't address his behavior - *because I loved him*.

I now have a much healthier and accurate understanding of love. What I have learned about love and what I share with my clients is this:

Love doesn't mean I'm a doormat,

Love doesn't mean I have to say yes,

Love doesn't mean I won't get upset,

Love doesn't mean I have to support what I don't believe in,

Love doesn't mean I have to buy you everything you want,

Love doesn't mean I'll always agree with you and

Love doesn't mean I accept disrespectful or volatile behavior.

Love means I seek to understand and communicate that understanding to the other person,

Love means I respectfully express my feelings and perspectives.

Love means I set an example of what it means to respect and treat others,

Love means I adjust my parenting style to fit each child's needs and

Love means I express and model positive attention.

Loving too much looks like:

- Telling "white lies" to our children instead of truth
- Rescuing our sons instead of teaching responsibility
- Taking responsibility for things they should do themselves
- Fighting their battles and sheltering them from situations
- Always giving in
- Giving excessively
- Being too permissive
- Bribing them to get them to do what you want

Loving "too" much indicates that the "giver" surrender their needs, wants, and desires for those of the "receiver" in hopes the "receiver" will reciprocate with the affirmation, affection, and attention, forever. It is essentially conditional and equates to emotional bribery on the part of the "giver."

Healthy mother/son Love looks like:

- Establishing your role as parent
- Training them through example, instruction and discipline
- Setting healthy boundaries
- Helping them take responsibility for their actions
- Teaching them consequences
- Practicing active listening as a communication method
- Teaching them how to express their emotions and modeling it
- Giving them clear standards and providing them with intentional ways to stretch and be challenged for character growth and development

Learning Self-Love

What is apparent is that, as mothers of sons we can tend to have a warped sense of love because of our own lack of true self-love. While we can express and defend our love for our sons, we do not see the necessity to do the same for ourselves. We tend *not* to practice this same commitment to loving ourselves that we have to loving them. This creates an imbalance, and sets us up to extend to our sons a facsimile of love, but not real love.

When we are not taught the importance of self-love, as a basis of our human relationships, and how to love all of ourselves - our size, our weight, our looks, our abilities, our flaws, and mistakes -

we will form a low self-image of ourselves. In turn, this becomes low self-esteem and lowered self-value. We then create an unhealthy, dependent understanding and we then express and seek love that affirms and validates our warped understanding.

This leaves us susceptible to forming unhealthy relationships where we are disrespected, used, abused or we feel like we have to earn love or prove our love. This behavior usually spills over to our relationship with our sons. What I have found is that if we can start seeing the link between the unhealthy patterns, habits, and situations in our approach to parenting our sons, and their relationship to low-level self-love, we can begin to start making changes *on the inside* that that will ultimately create the shifts we desire *on the outside*, in our relationships.

Some mothers have major holes in their self-love. Many mothers expect their sons to be the man they secretly desire for themselves in a romantic relationship. *It is almost perverse.* This behavior can even be witnessed in the terms of endearment we assign to our sons such as: my everything, my king, my life, daddy, my man, my ride or die, my number one, my day one, and the list goes on. I've heard them all. These are all terms that should be appropriately used with adult boyfriends and husbands, but not a child. I find that women who refer to their sons this way also long for men to complete or validate them. They have yet to find completeness within themselves and believe that without a man, they are incomplete. This disposition is a direct result of low self-esteem and lack of self-love. Take the Self-Love Test below to get a clear understanding of where you are with your level of self-love.

Self-Love Test

Answer the questions below, Yes or No, to help gauge your level of self-love.

1. Do you constantly compare yourself to others?
2. Do you talk negatively about your body either internally or out loud?
3. Do you find yourself staying in relationships where you are mistreated or disrespected?
4. Do you let fear drive your decisions?
5. Do you put on a mask to hide your vulnerability?
6. Do you hide your feelings or opinions to appease others?
7. Do you have a hard time saying No to others?

If you responded Yes to 3 or more questions, there is the need for a big upgrade in your level of self-love. Immediate attention and change is needed to help you raise your level of self-love.

You can raise your level of self-love by making a few small changes such as:

1. Practicing positive self-talk
2. Exercising

3. Not beating yourself up when you make a mistake
4. Doing more of what you enjoy
5. Surrounding yourself with positive people
6. Celebrating yourself
7. Not comparing yourself to others
8. Engaging in intentional "forgiveness work" to begin to "clear" negative emotions from your mind, body and spirit

Unconscious Stunting

When my son became a teenager, I started to notice that he seriously struggled to communicate his frustrations without lashing out, crying or throwing things. While he always seemed to have issues with anger as a child, I chalked it up to it being normal for a young boy. I always thought he would grow out of it.

This wasn't the case. In fact the tantrums got worse and he began hitting walls and running away whenever he was told No. He didn't take feedback well and was quick to point out others' mistakes whenever his behavior was in question. He didn't take responsibility for his actions, without blame, constant rationalization, and justification. Because I gave him everything he wanted and he didn't have to earn a thing, he didn't know how to work for what he wanted and nor did he know how to handle rejection. He displayed two emotions: anger and sadness. And even though he was extremely funny and could make others laugh, I hardly saw him genuinely happy. He was extremely sensitive and cried whenever he was angry or disappointed. He didn't receive feedback well at all and took everything too personally. I believe these tantrums and "fits of anger" were a direct by-product of his stunted emotional development.

The mothers I've interviewed report the same emotional behaviors being displayed by their sons. Because their sons weren't used to hearing the word No, they, in turn, couldn't handle disappointments, failure, feedback or rejection well at all. As a result, they often got angry when told no and at times would even exhibit violent behavior. They took feedback very personally because they weren't accustomed to having their behavior questioned or were used to being bailed out by their mothers. As a result, they struggled with respecting those in positions of authority, such as teachers, principals, and even law enforcement.

Reflection

As a mother, I know that you desire the best for your children, even if you've made some mistakes along the way. If you feel alone and don't feel you have the support you need, I want you to know that you're not alone and I am here to support you. We do not intentionally set out to over love, s-mother or stunt the growth of our sons and most times this is done unconsciously. You still have time to break this cycle. Start now by learning to love yourself, acknowledging the unhealthy behaviors I've been illuminating, and choosing to make new and different choices.

Reflection Questions

1. What behaviors does your son exhibit that indicate his emotional development may be stunted?
2. What thoughts and behaviors of your own would you say have contributed to this?
3. Read 1 Corinthians 13:4-7. In what ways can you show this type of love first to yourself? To your son?

Chapter 3

"The Boyfriend/Husband Replacement"

As soon as the doctor yelled out, "It's a boy!" he became "my little man." He was the answer to my prayers. I was determined to show everybody how a mother raises her son and how a man should treat a woman. This was my chance to mold him into the "perfect man." I had the crazy expectation that he somehow, would take the place of all the males in my life. In my mind, he was tee'd up to be my substitute boyfriend! In my twisted thinking, as long as I had him in my life, I didn't need anyone else. Here's how the scenario, or more accurately, the fantasy went in my head. When I was lonely, he'd entertain me; when I was hurt, he'd comfort me; when I was happy, he'd celebrate with me; and when I was angry, he'd soothe me.

I met my husband Raymond when KB was two years old. Prior to this, I dated someone for a short time who then dumped me, stating that he didn't want to be a father. I hadn't asked him to be nor did I want him to be. In my mind, KB was mine, and frankly I didn't want any man, even his biological father, telling me how to raise *my* son. This is one of the reasons I never pursued child support. I was going to do this *on my own*. So when my husband came along and asked *me and KB* out on a date, I took notice. We walked around Greenlake in Seattle. KB's little legs grew tired and my date graciously offered to carry him on his neck. KB wasn't having that and scowled at him while clinging to my leg. This behavior continued, even after Raymond had become his stepfather, and it continued throughout his 19 years. Sure, they had some good times. He started calling Raymond "Dad" at the age of three but KB never truly accepted another man loving his mother. He was used to being the only "man" in my life and Raymond interrupted this. Because my son was essentially "my man," Raymond threatened KB's influence and position with me. KB wasn't interested in sharing me with another man and had no intention of me loving another man. Even at the young age of two, he displayed his jealously almost the instant they met.

Raymond was not only a threat because he had influence over me and my decision-making in regards to KB, he also received my love, affection, and attention; all which had once solely been only his domain. As a single mother, KB and I were inseparable. We held hands, hugged, and kissed each other (on the cheek or a short peck) often. All which seemed appropriate, but we had gotten used to the affection of one another, and we were dependent on it after a bad day at work or daycare or when we didn't feel well. So, when Raymond started getting my affection it became a problem for KB. He became jealous of Raymond, and often I was made to feel like I was choosing one over the other.

KB rebelled by not listening to Raymond and by rebuking his love. He wasn't at all shy about voicing his disdain for Raymond. He constantly made me choose between the two of them, and nine out of ten times, he won out. Whenever Raymond disciplined him, he would go to his room and call me down to his room. He would be steaming mad at me for "allowing" Raymond to discipline him and for me not stopping it. To please KB, I would go to Raymond and ask him to alter his original decision. Raymond did it begrudgingly and often reacted just as KB did.

I didn't care, as long as KB was happy, I was happy, because this kept me being the "cool mom." I even had fantasies about how his relationships with girls would be. We would be good friends, and we would all get along and do everything together. She couldn't love him without loving me too. In my mind, we were sharing him, and you couldn't love him without loving me - we were a package.

The boyfriend/husband replacement is a phenomenon when the mother elevates her son to the role of her boyfriend or husband in her mind and behavior. This manifests in several ways; by the way we communicate with him more as an equal and not a parent, how we forsake other male relationships because of our sons, and how our expectations for our sons are that of a boyfriend or husband.

This is common with some of the mothers I've interviewed. Of course, this isn't done purposely or even knowingly. More often it is a result of the mother's bad experiences with the father of her children, her own father or other romantic relationships in her life. Her frustrated or thwarted desires usually start with the notion that she doesn't want her son to be like any of these men. Then she tries to ensure that she begins to fall in love with the "good" man she's given birth to versus the "bad" ones she's been hurt by in the past. As the mother, she has authority over her son so she can literally make him do what she wants, including caring for her, spending time with her, cleaning for her and doing all the things she believes a man should do for her.

The Fall-out

Because I hadn't experienced much success in relationships with men in my own past, I had many fantasies of how a perfect relationship should be. I unknowingly projected this longing on to my son. I wanted my son to be the type of man other women would kill for. I wanted him to be the epitome of the "perfect man" inside of the context of the "perfect" relationship I'd concocted in my mind. I set out to teach him how to care for and love women. How I taught him was by being the woman in the relationship. I would call him handsome, cute, and my everything. I had no qualms about him being the love of my life. I dressed him like a little man because he had to look good. He had to look like the man I desired for myself. The positive attention and comments he got as a child because of his outer appearance, made me feel special and validated. The comments and attention he got legitimized me, in my mind, and confirmed that yes, I had created the "perfect man."

When the son becomes a teenager, the effect of this dynamic is expressed through expectations for the son to be the provider, protector and assume responsibilities an adult partner would usually take on such as sharing household chores, playing the friend who listens, gives advice, and the unspoken expectations that many women desire a man to "just know" what needs to be done. If the mother believes a man's role is to provide for her, she will expect her son to be her provider, she will often give him a pass to skip school to work, earn money by illegal means and come and go as he pleases as long as her financial needs are met.

If the mother believes a man's role is to rescue or help them, their son will be expected to become her rescue. If the mother believes a man's role is to protect her, she will have an expectation for her son to be her protector and will demand he agree with her, stand up for her, and even become the "man of the house" by being her "security officer" at home. When mothers set out to create the ideal man *through* their sons, it always results in disappointment.

The effects of this dynamic can take on one or more of the following forms of expressions within the son:
1. He doesn't mature into an adult and will often stay with his mother well into his adult years.
2. He becomes a "Mama's boy" and finds it difficult to stay in relationships with women; OR

3. He resents mom for making him her provider, protector or rescuer or being overly emotionally dependent upon him, and as soon as he turns eighteen, he leaves home. However, the son usually has a strained relationship with his mom thereafter.

This is debilitating to the psyche of a young man. The sons who are overly dependent on their moms will often feel attacked when critiqued, and/or they are emotionally immature. Their self-worth will rise and fall based upon what they have and whether or not they have a love interest(s). For example they may seek to date women outside of their ethnicity and class to prove they are worthy. For the sons who resent their mother, they will hide their true feelings, be hot tempered, and are apt to struggle with intimacy, trust and commitment. This is because as a child they couldn't express their own needs and desires which caused a hatred for women to grow within them.

I met a young man who resented his mother for the expectation she had of him to be "her man." He was made to take her everywhere and was expected to drop everything and be there for her whenever she needed him. She would give him the silent treatment and would change her number if he didn't call her enough. She attempted to use guilt to get him to do things for her. He was finally able to set some boundaries with her by sharing with her his true feelings, asserting himself as an adult who was entitled to his own opinion, and by making it clear what he would do when he felt disrespected, used or mistreated. Doing this, he broke free from her attachment to him and unhealthy dependence on him.

Reflection

If you realize you have been doing this, please don't beat yourself up. I encourage you to start taking baby steps, understanding that things will change with practice and time. Be patient with yourself as you make these changes. I recommend you have an honest conversation with your son, and the two of you create new healthy expectations. Don't be afraid to seek outside help or support for yourself, your son or to help with facilitating a conversation between the two of you.

Reflection Questions

1. Take an honest inventory of your current relationship with your son. Where are you unconsciously requiring him to fulfill the role of the missing man or husband in your life?
2. Where have you found yourself pushing your desires on your son, instead of nurturing and bringing out his natural gifts and talents?
3. What term(s) of endearment do you have for your son?
4. Reflect and write down what meaning(s) this moniker holds.
5. Does the moniker's meaning create a healthy expectation of your son, feed a fantasy, or create a feeling of heaviness or burden for him?

Chapter 4
Rebellion

The day after Christmas in 2006 at the age of 13, KB was jumped and robbed by gunpoint outside of a shopping mall. The young men took his expensive North Face jacket, his brand-new Jordan tennis shoes and his PSP portable game, all which were Christmas gifts. He came home scared, sad, and embarrassed. This day changed the trajectory of my son's life. That was the day he decided that he needed protection, and that protection was in the form of joining a gang. I felt helpless. I felt like my baby was forced to grow up that day once he was faced with some real danger. It was almost like a loss of a certain level of his innocence and he was no longer sheltered from violence.

After this incident I noticed a drastic change in KB's behavior. While I was used to him talking back and getting angry, I still could depend on him to go to school, get good grades, do his chores, and come home by curfew. But this particular year he started hanging out with boys I didn't know, boys who looked like trouble and he started to frequently request to spend the night at a certain friend's house across town.

That next year when he came home for Christmas vacation from Dallas, he was hell bent on spending all his time with his friends who lived across town. In June of 2008 after being back home from Dallas for just two weeks, he ran away from home for the first time. It was because Raymond told him he couldn't go to his friend's house. I was so scared and didn't know what was going on with him. In what seemed like only a matter of , my baby was becoming someone I didn't recognize. I had surgery the day he ran away and was heartbroken when his father came to visit me without him. I just knew he would come see me at the hospital, but he didn't.

One evening he wanted to go to the other side of town to attend a party and I agreed to drive him. On the way there Raymond called and forbid him to go. He was so angry that he attempted to jump out of the car while we were on the freeway. Later we found out his friend was killed at that party; a friend I didn't know. A few months earlier, a friend of his was gunned down outside of a restaurant. This made two of his new friends that had been killed in a matter of months. *What was going on with my son?* The deaths of his two friends had a huge impact on him. He was more and more, becoming a person who was increasingly angry, distant, and withdrawn.

That Fall he was registered for tenth grade. My prayer was that once school started and he made the basketball team, that everything would come back together. This wasn't the case. KB didn't make it home from Dallas in time for basketball tryouts and wasn't able to play. This devastated him.

He began skipping school, coming home late and running away more often. I would drop him off to school just for him to leave and hang out at a friend's house most of the school day. I did everything in my power to keep him in school. He ended up at an alternative school, which only lasted a week or so. Before I knew it, my son was a high school dropout. Up until this point, I was at his school almost every day, meeting with the school officials, trying to get help. I was exhausted, frustrated, and scared.

Soon thereafter, I found out he was smoking marijuana and also carrying a gun. One evening he was attempting to come home to get some clothes after being gone for a week and my husband wouldn't let him in the house. An argument ensued and he pulled a gun on my husband. This was his first trip to Juvenile Detention and his first felony charge. I was in denial. I didn't share this with many people. My husband and I were constantly arguing over how to handle him. I feared for his life and couldn't sleep at night.

I was referred to a gang intervention program that sent two male caseworkers to my home. In my conversation with them is when we found out KB was in a gang. He joined when he was thirteen. That day my life turned upside down. *How did this happen?* My baby, the basketball star, the sensitive handsome well-dressed boy

I was raising, was now *in a gang*??!! My behavior towards him changed. I wanted my baby back. Every chance I got, I voiced my disappointment with him. I constantly demanded that he pull his pants up, comb his hair, and go to school. I barely recognized my son. My relationship with my husband got further strained. I only confided in my sister and this secret became harder and harder to hide and keep.

The women at my church would hear rumors and confront me. Former basketball coaches and family would tell me they saw him on the streets with his pants sagging, smelling like weed. I became more and more embarrassed. As he continued to change right before my eyes, I was forced to start looking at myself and my mothering. I could no longer avoid what was right in front of my eyes. *What did I miss?* This *wasn't* how I planned it, how I dreamt it would be for him, for us. This was the same feeling I had when, after giving 10 years to a man, the relationship ended with nothing. No commitment. Nothing to show for all of my hard work and time invested.

Denying the Signs

All the signs were there but I couldn't seem to face them. My baby wasn't the little rambunctious cutie pie I knew him to be. His behavior grew more violent, angrier, and more defiant. I no longer had his ear and I couldn't "make" him do anything. There were countless nights that I didn't know where he was, and then when he *was* home, he was asleep. Once he awakened, he was ready to hit the streets. The arguing between he and his stepfather grew worse as did my relationship with my husband. Raymond wanted him out of the house and I wanted him home. I believe at some point, my husband grew tired of me not allowing him to discipline KB the way he saw fit, so he stopped trying.

Many mothers will undermine the attempts of the adult male, whether the biological father or stepfather, to discipline their son by having secret agreements with her son to give him money, to drive him places and to lift the restriction, despite what the male has said. The male however, is made to feel ganged up on, and will soon give up. And the son will lose respect for the other male.

In my mind's eye, I chose to keep trying to see my son as the innocent little boy he once was. In doing so, I ignored the signs that were right in front of me. I kept thinking, *"This is just a phase."* I kept praying that it would end just as quickly as it began. As much as I tried to avoid the truth, it was right in front of my face. My son was becoming someone I didn't know nor did I like.

The advice I received felt so judgmental that I wasn't interested in hearing what others had to say. So I ignored it or dismissed it. I had poured my entire life into my son, or so it felt, and I didn't want to hear what anyone had to say about my parenting or how he was turning out. So I decided not to talk to anyone about my son and tried to handle it all on my own. BIG MISTAKE. In doing so, I continued to relate to him from the delusional belief that he was still the same "good" child who was going to school, getting good grades, and honoring his curfew. I would still take him where he wanted to go, buy him what he wanted, and give him money when he needed it. This doesn't mean that I didn't yell at him about his choices, beg him to change, try to make him feel guilty about his behavior and threaten to kick him out. He knew, just as I did, that these were all empty threats.

If you have or are experiencing these types of things with your son, I understand. I know how it feels to not know what to do, to not know where else to turn or who you can trust, to feel helpless, even powerless, to change what you see happening to your son before your very eyes.

The first thing I suggest is that you don't judge yourself. This will keep you in denial. Then make getting your son's attention about his behavior the important thing. Find help from your community, your church, family services, a friend, mentor, counselor, or a family member. Be kind to yourself during this time as you will have to tell the frustrating story about your son over and over until you get the help you need.

Running from the Truth

Even though I knew in my heart my son was in trouble, I didn't want to hear it from others including my husband. At that time, I was incapable of not internalizing their advice. Any feedback, and especially criticism was met with resistance and painful feelings of blame – self-blame. I wanted to avoid hearing *anything* that suggested my mothering maybe flawed, unhealthy or disabling.

This is what I find to be true with other mothers as well. It can be difficult for us to accept the truth about our sons without feeling like we are bad mothers. After all, if it's only us trying to raise them, without the active support and presence of the father, then not only are we angry with the father, but we can be angry with ourselves. Denial seems the less painful option.

Reflection

As hard as it may be to hear, the only way you can change what's happening is to face the truth about you, your parenting and your son's behavior. A wise woman once told me to make sure I exhausted all the possibilities to save my son, so that God forbid, if something happened to him, I could rest knowing I had done everything I could. I give you the same advice. Be creative. How can you involve the men in your life? How can you facilitate them coming together to mentor and guide your son? Because my son loved basketball I asked coaches and other players to help me. I asked my Pastor to write him when he was in detention. I asked men I knew who were former gang members to talk to him. Resolve not to give up until you are satisfied you've tried everything.

Reflection Questions

1. What truths have you been avoiding about your parenting? About your son?

2. What/Who are resources for you that support your son getting the help he needs?

Defending his Unacceptable Behavior

I heard about my son's troubling behavior from every direction – from friends, family, my husband, the court, school, his friends, and neighbors. It felt like a nightmare. It wasn't like I didn't see it. That wasn't the case at all – there were the sleepless nights, the crying, the praying, the constant arguing with my husband, and the embarrassment. I knew damn well something was going on. Regardless of his behavior, *that was my baby*, and my job as a mother was to defend him. I saw his potential, his heart and his innocence and it was because of these things I never lost hope in who he could be.

What I now realize is that I chose to constantly defend my son because it was more so about defending myself. I was insulating and protecting myself. I was defending the fact that I made the best choices I knew how to make at the time, though these choices were too often from a place of my own woundedness, "unhealedness" and residual emotional wounds from my own childhood. In my mind, acknowledging that something was wrong meant that I had done something wrong. That was too painful to face so I didn't face it. It was as if I was on trial, my parenting, my decisions and my behavior were on trial, too. When I look back now, the truth is that I wasn't strong enough at the time, to separate his behavior from my identity as his mother. I even had someone ask me what did I do to my son to make him the way he was. In my mind, this question validated my belief that when others looked at my son's behaviors, they judged me negatively.

Many mothers are right where I was. While it is true that a mother's decisions or lack thereof do have a direct reflection on her child's behavior, accepting bad behavior doesn't mean that you are a bad person or that your intentions didn't come from a pure place. What I find is that our intentions usually often come from a broken, hurt or unrealistic place, resulting in allowing bad behaviors to go unaddressed, denied, minimized or ignored.

Reflection Questions

Think back to a time you were told about your son's poor behavior.

1. What was your initial response?
2. Did you default to defending him? What was your justification, in your mind?
3. How can you respond in a way that you hold him responsible for his behavior without feeling judged?

Suffering in Silence

What I had desperately hoped was that this was just a phase my son was going through, and thus, there was no reason to get others involved. In my mind it was going to change just as quickly as it had begun. He often mentioned to me how he hated hearing me tell my friends about the challenges I was having with him. I could see from the look on his face that he felt I was tattling on him. I didn't want to betray him by sharing with others what he was doing. This was our business and no one needed to know.

I got very good at keeping secrets. For more than a year, I dealt with the reality of my son becoming someone I didn't know anymore. Of course my husband knew, but he and I didn't talk much about it, otherwise an argument would ensue. The more we talked about it, the more we argued, and the more our relationship became strained. So it was a topic we avoided like the plague. Or more accurately, like a big purple trumpeting elephant in the middle of the room. I told my twin sister a few things but couldn't find it within myself to tell her everything. I went to work every day as if nothing was happening at home. I managed a team of 55 people, and none of them had any idea about what I was dealing with at home. I also became an ordained minister during this time. I attended church every Sunday even though I was angry at God. I wondered where He was during all of this madness. I thought my perfect church attendance, my involvement in *every* ministry, my prayers, my preaching and my service would have solidified and guaranteed me a perfect child and a perfect life. So I kept up appearances and acted as if everything was just fine. Even those closest to me didn't know that, secretly, I was suffering in silence and crying myself to sleep most nights. The guilt and shame ran deep within me.

Many of the mothers I see are referred to me by their friends or family after they hear my story. What is clear to me is that these mothers are suffering in silence. Often, to their friends and family, it seems as if they are ignoring the problem. The fear of judgment is usually the #1 reason mothers aren't open to discussing their son's behaviors with others. This is mainly because these mothers are often carrying shame, overwhelm, frustration, and they fear judgment and potential condemnation.

When I meet with them and share my story, including my truths, they are relieved to know that they no longer have to suffer in silence. They are relieved that they now have someone to talk to who understands, and most importantly, who won't judge them.

So if this is something you have struggled with, or still do, you are not alone. I invite you to choose a different way of handling this, but please do it now, and before it's too late. I invite you to consider that it might be much more than a passing phase or something temporary, and open your mouth, to speak up to those who have success in this area, have triumphed in this area, and are capable of support, help, encouragement, and/or wise counsel.

Fear of Judgment

I define judgment in this context in two ways; 1) as someone determining what I do or have done as right or wrong or good or bad based on their opinion. If their opinion is that I am bad or wrong then this judgment is an attack on my identity. For example, if I am told that my son's behavior is bad, I then attach that judgment to my identity and conclude that I must be a bad parent; 2) Someone determines another's negative fate or future based on their past or present behavior. For example, your son will never amount to anything if they keep hanging out with those types of people. The damage of the first form of judgment was self-condemnation, and the damage of the second form of judgment was condemning my son.

Because of my fear of being judged this way, I chose not to ask for help, admit there was a problem, or discuss with others what was going on with my child. Instead I chose to defend his behavior. This seemed to be the safest thing to do to avoid being judged and to avoid having my greatest fears about my son visited upon me. My experience at the time was that though I may not have been discussing what was going on, it was no secret that others were still gossiping behind my back and making negative judgments about me and me and my son.

I was working at a management level for the court system and was extremely careful not to share the details of my rebellious son's life with my co-workers. This was difficult – I had to carefully edit my responses and conversation so as not to divulge the truth about my son. When I started this career, my son was just a year old and many of them had watched him grow up, so it wasn't unusual for them to ask about him. By the time he was 15, I got good at lying and pretending as if everything was okay. But once he entered the court system, I could no longer keep my secret. I was attending court with my son in full view of some of the judges I was on committees with and employees I managed. I feared what my employees and co-workers would say about me once they found out. I feared judgment that came with them knowing my son wasn't the little innocent boy they once knew, and I wasn't the manager they had come to admire and respect.

Guilt and Shame

Besides the fear of being judged, the guilt and shame is what kept me lying, avoiding and pretending. Witnessing first-hand the impacts and effects my parenting had on my son was profoundly painful. And it was only exasperated by the rumors and the gossip that was taking place. But the constant negative comments and whispering from others made it worse. Little did they know I was already harshly judging myself and their judgments only made me feel worse.

I already felt horribly guilty because I hadn't taken the advice of my husband. I had undermined his discipline for so long. I felt ashamed that as a manager within the court system, a minister and a mentor to youth, that my own son wasn't growing up as I had hoped and expected. I also felt like a fraud because I was helping *other* youth but didn't seem to be able to help my own son. I had coddled my son, catered to his every need and whim, and elevated him above my husband and even my own needs. It was deeply painful to look where it got me.

The Confrontation

I had an awful experience of being confronted by five young girls I was mentoring through a mentoring program associated with my church. They got together to tell me that they could no longer follow my teachings because of my son's behavior. Because my son was out of control, I had no right to tell them how to live their life, they felt. What hurt more was that my adult peers within the organization knew this confrontation was going to take place and had approved it.

This confrontation felt like a public shaming and made me feel even more guilty about my son's behavior. I will never forget how I felt driving home from the mentoring meeting that night. It was bad enough that my son was becoming someone I no longer knew but to have it thrown in my face by teenagers and the adults within an organization that I gave so much time and energy to made me feel rejected and abandoned at a time when I already felt so much guilt and shame.

In meeting with mothers, I find that I'm not the only one who has been confronted about their son's behavior. Friends and family tend to think that the confrontation will force the mother to see the error of her ways. However, these usually never go well and instead make the mother retreat, vowing not to tell a soul about her son or her feelings. The mothers I've spoken to who have had similar confrontations only heard that they are bad mothers who are wrong in how they parented their sons.

Reflection

What would have helped me at the time is to have been able to move through a series of questions about my son. This is something I use in my coaching and facilitation sessions with mothers. I guide the mother through a series of questions about herself and the story she is telling herself about what is going on with her son. It is much deeper than "You let him do whatever he wants" and "That's why he doesn't listen to you or anyone else." The way to help a mother is to help her recognize the *root* of why the behavior has occurred instead of over-focusing on the behavior itself. I began to pray for myself instead of only him and asked God to reveal the root of what was going on with me and how I could change. I opened up to my husband and asked him to hold me accountable. I relinquished sole ownership of discipline and supported my husband as the new disciplinarian. I began seeking counseling and counsel from others. I came out of hiding. I recommend you do the same. There are people waiting to support you!

Reflection Questions

1. List one person you trust and are comfortable with their feedback about how you parent your son.
2. Where are you resisting advice or help because you fear judgment?
3. What judgment about yourself do you fear?

4. How have you been able to separate observations or advice about your son's behavior from an attack on your character as a mother?

To Mothers Raising Sons

Chapter 5
"Falling out of Love" with Your Son

It was a reality check similar to when you finally come to terms with a cheating man and realize the thrill is gone. One day I looked at my sixteen-year-old son and saw someone I could barely stand. His sagging pants, he reeked of marijuana, his conversation was full of slang and swearing and continually seeing him in a detention visiting room began to disgust me. I grew tired of begging him to change, going to court, picking him up late at night at bus stops, wondering where he was, getting calls from the school, fearing calls from the police and even worse, a coroner. *I gave up.* I stopped trying to win him over with kindness and I let him go. I let him live the life that seemed to be calling him and the streets that beckoned him. I no longer lied about what was going on and I no longer spoke of him as if he was doing okay. I told the truth and I didn't care what others said or thought. I gave him to God and I prayed that God would keep him safe.

He didn't like being around me anymore. Instead of encouraging him and begging him to be better I started talking about him and telling him what would happen if he stayed on this path. I no longer hid my true feelings in order for him to like me or to do what I asked. I was done and he knew it. I still gave him money and I still attended court but I had come to terms with who he actually was instead of who I wanted him to be.

I was deeply angry with him. Frankly, I felt like he betrayed me. I had given him everything he ever wanted and *this was how he repaid me?!* I had been shamed by those closest to me; I was made to feel guilty for my actions and I was embarrassed by those I worked with - *all because of him. I was mad.* Everything I had worked so hard for crumbled right before my eyes. I was faced with the truth and I didn't like it. The only thing I could do was to let him go. I gave up on him.

Grieving the "Old" Son

Letting my son go felt like a death had occurred. I had to let go and grieve the son I believed and hoped would someday be a college graduate, a handsome mild mannered boy who was respectful, had no criminal record and who was gainfully employed. I had to face the fact that he wasn't going to be a basketball star and might never even graduate high school. All of this devastated me and left me feeling like a failure. But in order for me to move forward I had to let go of who I wanted him to be and accept who he was. This didn't mean I condoned his behavior, it just meant that I had to come to terms with the fact that he was not the idyllic young boy I had continued to imagine in my fantasies about the perfect son. He was making decisions for himself, and what I wanted for him no longer seemed to matter. He even told me that there came a point when he no longer cared what I thought and that made it possible for him to make the decisions that got him in trouble and led him down a path to destruction.

I remember the moment when I looked at the pictures of a young KB hanging in my home and in my office. For the first time I realized this KB no longer existed. I had been, for so long, trying to preserve this little boy and in doing so I couldn't see the KB that was forming right before my eyes. In my heart, he was still an impressionable and innocent little boy who loved his mother. But in reality, he was a rebellious teenager who was making his own decisions, and bad ones.

Letting Go of your Fantasy

Every time I looked at his basketball trophies and the pictures of the young KB, I was faced with the truth that this was no longer the son I was raising. Because KB dropped out of school in the tenth grade and he didn't take pictures his freshman year. The last formal picture I had of him was as an eighth grader. He looked so sweet and innocent. He was the epitome of my fantasy - handsome, smart, talented, and funny. Unknowingly, I chose to see him as if in a "freeze frame" like this when visiting him in detention and sitting with him in court. This was why it was hard for me not to defend him and to admit he was in trouble. I held on to that fantasy for as long as I could. But one day my eyes were opened and I had to let go of the fantasy and accept him for who he had become.

I believe this is one of the hardest things for a parent to do, especially a mother who has fantasized for so long about who she wanted her son to become, and the way she wanted to see him grow up and develop. Letting go of this fantasy becomes the equivalent of accepting and recognizing that the man of your dreams will never come to rescue you. It is also the feeling that all your hard work and effort was in vain.

I have heard many mothers tell the story of how they made huge sacrifices, lost both friendships and romantic relationships, spent loads of money and invested countless hours. They often come right back to the question: *"This is how he repays me?"* A mother sees the outcome as a personal attack on her love and efforts, similar to that of a romantic relationship gone sour. The fantasy then turns into disappointment with both herself and her son.

Being Disappointed with our Sons

I became very disappointed with my son. My disappointment towards him soon turned into anger. I was angry because he was committing crimes. I was angry because he was in a gang. It was this anger that helped me to let him go. It was as if I no longer liked him. He had everything he wanted and more, and I couldn't understand why he would chose to drop out of school, leave home and live a life of crime, and mischief. *I was heartbroken.* I was disappointed that he didn't continue his basketball career and that he let himself go. My disappointment towards him created an inner conflict for me. How could I love someone that I didn't like? He was supposed to be the perfect man and instead he became the man of my nightmares. As his mother I still had the obligation to raise him. While I let him go in theory, I still struggled with my desire to please him and my inability to say No. This caused me to say one thing and do another. This frustrated my husband and made me even more disappointed with my son. I was risking my relationship for him and he didn't seem to appreciate it.

I was becoming furious with him. He continually made poor decisions. Every time I got a call from a police office or the juvenile detention staff, I was infuriated. His chosen lifestyle was getting old to me. My disappointment towards him made it easier for people to give me advice: they would suggest that I kick him out of the house, change the locks, or take his cell phone. Even though he infuriated me, I still wasn't ready to do these things because I feared for his safety. This same excuse allowed him to come in and out of my life, and the house, at his discretion. In my anger, I would try harder and harder to get him to do better but the more I nagged, the more he stayed away. I was in a Catch-22, and frankly didn't know which way to go and how to break the cycle.

Reflection

To let go of the fantasy of who you hoped your son would be, start seeing him as who he is now, and based on this reality, set new expectations. Commit to rebuilding your relationship and accepting his uniqueness. Doing this will help you face your truth and come out of denial so you can get him the help he needs or adjust his responsibilities based on his maturity level. Consider a celebratory ritual to recognize and celebrate his growth. It can be an intimate gathering with family where you acknowledge his maturity and burn his old chore chart and create one that reflects his new level of responsibility.

Reflection Questions

1. What if any rituals do you have to acknowledge your son maturing?
2. How have you adjusted his responsibility to reflect his maturity level?

Chapter 6

How to Love Him

When You Don't Like Him Anymore

Grace

By 2009, he was now 16, and I had experienced over a year of my son in and out of my home, running away, smoking weed, taking multiple trips to juvenile detention and becoming someone I didn't like anymore. He and my husband were fighting more and my husband and I were constantly disagreeing about how to discipline him. We were always at odds with what each of us believed was the best way to discipline him. This made my home volatile, cold and tense. It was getting harder to pretend everything was okay and my faith was wavering. It got extremely hard for me to spend time with my son. If he wasn't asking for something, he was using street slang, a language that I didn't understand, or we were arguing about his new chosen lifestyle. Other times I was either in court with him or taking him to probation appointments. I spent so much time "supporting" him that it wore me out! I started to resent him. I felt used, I felt disrespected and I sure didn't feel loved.

I hate to admit it but I didn't like my son anymore. My entire life had been changed because of his behavior. Many nights I prayed it was all a dream and that we would get back to normal. The more time I spent in those detention visiting rooms and courtrooms, I was reminded of the truth that I tried so hard to hide from and my lack of parenting skills was thrown in my face. Everything I worked so hard for backfired and I was forced to look at the reality of my unhealed self and the impact it had on my parenting.

One day I was at work and a co-worker who I considered a friend asked me how things were going. This day, instead of sugar-coating the truth (I had gotten good at this), telling a lie or pretending everything was okay, I told the truth. Little did I know that she was experiencing some of the same behaviors with her teenage daughter. That day she uttered three words that changed my life! She said, *"Just Love Him!"* I didn't need clarification, or an explanation of how or any further instructions. I heard her loud and clear. At that moment I felt empowered, something I hadn't felt in two years.

This experience taught me the value of speaking my truth. If I hadn't have spoken up and told the truth, I wouldn't have received those three words that literally set me free from the bondage I was in. So many times, I had kept what I was going through a secret, for fear of shame and condemnation. As soon as I began to talk about it, from the pulpit and in one on one conversations, I was given the support, love, and encouragement I needed to get through this tumultuous season with my son. I learned I wasn't alone and I was encouraged to keep talking so that I could help other mothers come out from hiding.

My friend essentially told me to extend my son some grace. I define grace in this context as being able to see my son in a different light and seeing him past his behaviors, recognizing he was still a child that needed to be loved, understood and accepted. It was that experience that showed me what true grace looks and feels like. I re-opened my heart to him and, almost instantly, I began to love my son again even though I didn't like him. I did this by accepting him for who he was now and not who he *once* was or who I *wanted* him to be. I spent time trying to connect with him without the constant need to insert my feelings about his behavior, and instead of constantly nagging him every time he was home I started having conversations with him to get to know him, hear what he was thinking about and what he was going through. I chose to stop yelling at him to go to school, pull up his pants, and to stop gang banging. We were no longer at odds every moment of the day. Before I knew it, he started coming home. Love brought my son home. His behavior started to change and we started enjoying each other's company. Even though he was still doing things I didn't approve of, I chose to show him love despite his mistakes and decisions.

The biggest lesson I learned from this was not only how to extend my son grace, but to extend that same grace to myself. I had been punishing myself for my mistakes, judging myself for not parenting better. I was my own biggest judge and jury, and grace, released me from of my self-inflicted prison. It was this lesson that enabled me to hear similar stories from other mothers without passing judgment on them but instead being a safe place for them to share.

If you have been guilty of judging yourself. I want you to ask God to help you see yourself as He does. I want you to accept that despite any mistakes you may have made, you can start again. I understand changing your perspective about your son may take time, but I want to assure you that extending him grace will help to alter how you see him and ultimately alter the way he sees himself.

One of my clients reached out to me almost embarrassed to admit she didn't like her teenage son. He had begun talking back to her and asserting his need to be right in every conversation. She felt bad saying out loud that she didn't like him and she avoided spending time with him. Instead of letting him express his opinion, no matter how right or wrong he was, she constantly argued with him and let him know that he was neither right nor impressing her. This kept the two of them constantly at odds and unable to have a conversation without it escalating into an argument. My advice to her was to love him. I asked her to put less energy into arguing with him and asserting her desire to prove she was right, and put more energy into appreciating and encouraging his brilliance by letting him speak without interruption, encouraging him to take classes or to read books that would help to develop him into a bright young man and to compliment him when he gets good grades. Her role as his mother was to train him up by nurturing his gifts and talents and helping him discover how to use them. While she may not have liked how he demonstrated his intelligence, she was to use wisdom to help guide him in how to share his views, while understanding someone else's may be different than his. An example of this could be encouraging him to join the debate team.

Extending grace is about allowing our children to come into their own while still loving them, even when we may disagree. Extending grace to them gives them room to make mistakes without the constant need to punish, make them think and act like us, or turn out to become the profession or person who we believe they should be. Grace loves them even when we don't necessarily like them or their decisions.

Forgiving Him

One of the things I had to do was learn to forgive my son. I had taken his behavior as a personal affront. *"How could he do this to me after all I had done for him?"* I had grown bitter and resentful of him. Inside I felt like he had "turned on me." It seemed that every poor decision he made, I had allowed it to take root in *my* heart.

I made a deliberate decision to forgive him. I decided that in order for me to heal and for us to move forward, I had to forgive him. One day I wrote down all the things I needed to forgive him for and as I wrote them, I cried, I prayed, I screamed, and I began to release the resentment. This took me some time but after counseling and praying I was able to forgive him (see the prayers later on this chapter). I forgave him for dropping out of school, all the lies he told me, the countless hours I spent visiting him in detention, jail and prison, all the money I gave him, put on his books in jail, the fines, and restitution I paid on his behalf, the sleepless nights I stayed up worrying he would be killed, for all the tears I shed, for the guilt, shame and embarrassment, for the endless arguments and fights with Raymond.

I had an opportunity to release all of my hurt, disappointment, frustration, and anger using a process similar to the one I outline. I learned that forgiving him didn't release him from taking responsibility for his behavior or erase actual events that were in his past, but it freed me from the need to bring it up, yell, scream and literally beg him to own up to and admit he was wrong. Forgiving him allowed me to see and love him for who he was and not who I was trying to create. Forgiveness gave me the courage to tell my story, address my unhealedness and ultimately come out from hiding. This opened the door to a new relationship that was not based on my fantasies of who I wanted my son to be but on who he actually was. It lifted my heavy expectations of him of having to be the perfect man, the perfect son and my rescuer, and gave me the opportunity to find out who he was and what he desired for his life.

Forgiveness Activity

Preliminary steps: Grab your journal, find a quiet place. Take four deep breaths.

Reflect: Ask yourself these questions, specifically focused on your son, to get started:

> What are three painful situations related to my son I recall?
>
> What grudges against my son am I holding?
>
> What emotions are stirring within me?
>
> What resentments towards my son are weighing me down?
>
> What regrets do I have?
>
> What pain am I holding on to in regard to my son however recent or distant?
>
> What hurts do I have from each of these situations or events?

Identify Your Emotions: Identify the emotions that came up as you were completing the questions above and write them in the space below.

Forgive: Fill in the blanks below with the emotions you identified above.

What specific emotions resulted from this/these situations? List the emotions:

_____

_____

_____

I forgive *insert son's name* and release the *name the emotion*. Write this sentence repeatedly, for each of the situations, inserting a different one of the named emotions each time. You might have this sentence recurring on your paper or in your journal many times.

Release: Now, go back and READ, out loud each of the "I forgive" statements that you wrote. Write it down and say out loud the above forgiveness and release statement.

- You may find yourself vocally emotionally expressing yourself. Allow that.
- You will feel different feelings moving through you. Accept them. Feel them pass through.

Love: Express your love for your son by repeating I love you *insert his name* five times, out loud.

Forgiving Yourself

It wasn't enough to forgive him, I also needed to forgive *myself*. Because I harbored so much blame and guilt, it was pivotal for me to be able to release myself from taking sole ownership for my son's choices. I blamed myself for what went wrong with my son and for all of my issues, mistakes, and the blind eye I turned to him. I blamed myself for the wedge I created between him and my husband, Raymond. I blamed myself for his unhealthy emotions. I had to realize that I caused much of my own pain by blaming myself instead of allowing my son to own up to his decisions. In taking the sole blame I was buffering him and not allowing him to learn how to take responsibility for his actions. I had to forgive myself for all of this and create a new pattern in how we dealt with his behavior, not only so I could grow but so he could as well.

Once I forgave myself, I was able to transform our relationship to a much healthier one where both of us assumed responsibility. I was able to see clearly how my unhealthy understanding of love affected the way I chose to parent him. I was now able to discipline him without fear of abandonment. It was much easier for me to forgive him than to forgive myself. Forgiving myself required me to face truths about my parenting, the choices I avoided making that led up to situations with my son, my emotional health, my actual level of self-love, and my constant pattern of assuming blame for my son's behaviors. No matter how hard it was, I was committed to doing the forgiveness work and forgiving myself so that I could love him from a healthy place and not allow my guilt or my disabling beliefs to interfere with my role as his mother.

Forgiveness Prayer for You/Mother

Thank you for the gift You have given me in my son. Forgive me for the times I didn't recognize him as a gift, for resenting him when we didn't behave the way I wanted him to and for not seeing him as You see him. I ask that you heal the voids and empty places within me. Teach me to lead him and guide him in a way that is pleasing to You and to love him as You do.

Forgiveness Prayer for Your Son

Thank you for the gift You have given me in my son. Help me to extend him grace when he makes mistakes and to forgive him when he fails me. Teach me how to love him in a way that brings out his best and that demonstrates your love. Help me to keep my heart open even when I am disappointed or frustrated by his choices and behaviors.

Acceptance

Once I forgave him and myself I was able to see him beyond the criminal record, the clothes, the tattoos, and the behavior. I started to accept that this was who he chose to be. I was no longer embarrassed nor cared what others thought. I was able to accept his mistakes as his and not mine. This was a huge shift in my thinking. I no longer had the desire for him to be my ideal man or to fill the love void in my life. Accepting him freed me from this inner battle. Accepting him for who he was during this season of his life didn't mean that I lost hope of him having a bright, prosperous future. In fact, my faith in how God would use him grew stronger. I still believed God would use all of this for His good to help save other young men from the gang lifestyle. I still believed in my son and was still his biggest cheerleader.

Accepting our children for who they are and helping to uncover and develop their unique purpose is part of our assignment as mothers. If we try to train them up to be who we need them to be or who we think they should be, we miss the invitation to discover their life assignment and our role in helping them realize their divine purpose.

Our sons are gifts on loan to us from God. In fact, scripture says that sons are a reward. As a mother of a son God entrusted you with a gift. A mother's role is to:

- love and nurture her son,
- instill in him self-love and self-worth,

- teach him personal responsibility through discipline,
- show him how to be a good steward of his time, talent and treasure, AND
- teach him the importance of maintaining a healthy mind, body and soul.

Once I was able to release him from my expectations of *who* he *should* be and *how* he *should* be, and accepted him for who he was, I was able to have some peace and to see more clearly his life assignment and the purpose for which he was created.

Learning to Love the New Son

My son, now age 17, was growing up. I had been actively doing my forgiveness work, and learning to truly accept him. He started improving his behavior, he wasn't "hanging out" as much, and he was starting to dream more about his future. He had plans to own an auto repair shop. I was proud of who he was becoming. One Thursday morning in June 2010, he called me to surprise me with the news that he'd be graduating with his GED that Friday. I never thought I would be so happy about someone getting a GED. He had been taking classes, unbeknownst to me, as part of a program he attended while on probation. One thing I could say about KB was that he didn't miss a court date or a probation appointment. He made sure to take care of all that was required to do as part of his sentence.

Watching my son march down that aisle with his cap and gown at the age of seventeen, two years before he would have graduated from high school, made me so proud of him. It gave me hope - he was now making positive decisions in his life. I was ecstatic. I just knew that God had heard and answered my prayers. I started to see him in a different light, someone who was concerned about his future, his education, and who wanted to better himself.

I liked him again, not because of the GED accomplishment but because I was free from my guilt, my shame, and my attachment to depending upon him for my happiness. For the first time, I was able to love him for who he was and not who I wanted or needed him to be. I was able to love him regardless of his mistakes and shortcomings, and not for what I got in return. I was free and healed and that is what allowed me to love him again.

Reflection

Never lose hope in your son. Remain vigilant, available and loving. Know that by accepting him and letting him go, you are guiding him into adulthood.

Reflection Questions

1. In what areas do you to extend grace to yourself?
2. Where do you need to extend your son grace?
3. Write down 5 things you can do to get to know your "new" son.
4. What did you realize from the forgiveness exercise with your son?
5. What did you realize from the forgiveness exercise with yourself?

To Mothers Raising Sons

Chapter 7

Setting Boundaries

While I was enjoying this new relationship with my son, setting boundaries was necessary to ensure I didn't fall back into old patterns of allowing myself to be manipulated and used. I wasn't quite sure of how to do this without upsetting the new dynamic of our relationship, but I knew it needed to happen. One of the first boundaries I set was not allowing his friends and girlfriends to smoke, drink or party in my home. I also had to be sure to deal with any violations right away so that he knew I was serious and meant what I said. He had been so used to my bark being bigger than my bite. I had to take make sure to follow through with my consequences.

In the past he was always able to coerce me to change my mind and eventually I would cave in and grant him his wish, whatever that was. This made the transition to setting boundaries an extremely tough one for both of us; he was so used to me giving in and him getting his way. I had to be very intentional; I had to be very clear about what I would, and would not do, or put up with, and what the consequences would be if he didn't follow the rules. Because of his history with us, these would consist of just two, taking his cell phone and kicking him out of the house. While in the past I thought these were extreme, I now understood that I had to show him I was serious.

Because our relationship was so previously unhealthy, there were numerous boundaries that I had to put in place to re-establish my parental control. There would be no more swearing, yelling, demanding or using disrespectful tones with me or Raymond. Our cell phones were placed on Do-Not-Disturb at 11pm to keep him from interrupting our sleep by calling to ask for a late night ride. We gave him money with conditions he kept his curfew, did his chores and didn't get into trouble and we didn't jump in to fix everything he got himself into.

Setting these boundaries helped him see the correlation between his decisions and the consequences, taught him how to problem-solve, and to respect adults. These were all things that he didn't have to learn as long as I did everything for him. When a mom allows her son to undermine her authority, he will attempt to do this same thing with other adults in authority. I saw KB repeat this disrespectful behavior over and over with other adults such as teachers, coaches, police, and his stepfather. When he's able to "run over" his mom, a son will treat other adults with disrespect also, and even contempt.

I see many moms struggle with setting boundaries with their sons, especially when bad behavior was allowed to continue for so long. One client allowed her teenage son to smoke marijuana in her home because she thought it was better than having him do it on the street. She wanted to start enforcing a strict No Smoking policy in her home and was worried that he wouldn't adhere to her new boundary. I asked what her biggest fear was in enforcing this boundary. Like many moms she replied, "That he would be mad at me and not come home." Her response was tied to the belief that her son will only love her if he gets his way. As I was to discover, even this is connected to a deeper belief that she isn't loveable unless she sacrifices her own needs for another.

I challenged this mother to set *and keep* this boundary and to trust that it would work out. Often it is more the *fear of the* **reaction** *to setting the boundary* that keeps us from following through with it, than the setting of the boundary itself. I explained to her that she wouldn't know the response to setting a boundary until she set it. She did, and he was angry initially, but eventually he followed it. She is now working on setting boundaries in other relationships where this faulty belief has led to her accepting bad behavior in fear she would be rejected if she spoke up and spoke her truth.

I have found that mothers can have unconditional love for their sons but expect *conditional* love from their sons. This behavior often stems from the mother's unhealthy understanding of love. She can expect her son to demonstrate his love for her by performing, "Show me you love me," just as she expects from the men whom she has a romantic relationship with. If her son doesn't do what she asks or demands of him, she will believe he doesn't love her.

A mother who believes that you must "work for love" will not set boundaries as she believes doing this will be met with resistance and a withholding of love by her son. So instead she will give away her power and authority based on her belief that sacrificing her needs and her happiness for others is an act of love. In her mind, it guarantees that she will receive the love she desires from her son. However, again and again, this proves to be untrue

Learning to Say No

"No" was a word that was never used when it came to my son. Learning to say "No" to him wasn't an easy thing to do. I still had some fear that if I didn't give him what he asked for he would abandon me, that he would leave me, that I'd no longer be "his girl." But as a result of my forgiveness work and my renewed strength, I was determined to change this unhealthy pattern in my life not only with my son but with all the relationships in my life. I was presented with the perfect opportunity to practice using this new word. My son called and asked me for $2500 to buy a car. I knew that I had to say

No, and I did. Instead of him yelling at me, demanding it, or making me feel guilty, he said, "Okay" and hung up the phone. He never asked again and we continued on with our relationship. Everything I had feared did *not* manifest. I was overjoyed! Once I learned to say No it became easier and easier to do. I learned that my No didn't mean rejection of me by him, and it didn't mean that I loved him any less.

The more I said No the more he was determined to earn his own money. This proved challenging with his criminal history but it warmed my heart that he had regained hope and belief in himself. He started thinking about opening his own business and going to trade school. My saying No was what he needed to stop depending on others, especially me and other women, to give him money, and buy him nice things.

I work with a lot of mothers who struggle with saying No because they are fearful of their son's reaction, the need to feel wanted, a fear of his rejection, or because of their need for their son's dependency. If a mother doesn't create healthy boundaries and rewards her son regardless of his efforts or behavior, as he matures, he will believe that his unacceptable behavior is okay. The message he receives tells him that he can manipulate and use women to get what he wants. He can then become chronically dependent upon women for his financial livelihood.

Reflection Questions

1. Where do you need to say No to your son?
2. Write down 3-5 different ways to say No without saying No (e.g., "Yes, with conditions," "Let's discuss it," "Not now")

Letting Him Go

What does it mean to let your son go? Letting go is releasing him from your constant financial, spiritual, emotional, and physical dependency. Mothers are faced with letting their son go because they have to become an adult, it is necessary for the health of the parent, and the maturity of the son.

It is natural for a mother to be reluctant to release her son and let him go into the world to make their own decisions as an independent adult. However, this is something we tend not to do. When my son left home to move in with a friend, my heart was broken. I took it very personally. What was hard about letting go was having to fill the void of perceiving myself as the #1 woman in his life. I no longer had the same extent of control or influence over my son. I still saw him as "Mine." The thought of him living with someone else even stirred up feelings of jealousy. Even though it was one of his guy friends. I still felt betrayed. I still saw him as "my baby" who needed my love, protection, and provision.

Again, I wanted to be in control, and the more he aged and matured, my control over him lessened. I grieved, no longer feeling like I was needed. I missed his calls for my advice that made me feel special and valued. I missed his presence and energy in my house. I had dedicated my life to him and it felt like it was easy for him to walk away or "walk out on me." He was no longer dependent on me and I realized how much I secretly liked that. I had become dependent on his love to make me feel like I had succeeded at something. I had some hard questions to come to terms with: *Now where would my feelings of success come from? Who was I now that being a mother was no longer my number one priority?* Many mothers consider the relationship with their son as their only success, especially if they haven't experienced success in other male relationships or enough success in their own lives. My success was wrapped up in my son and when it was time to let him go, I grieved.

One of my clients has a similar story. Her son moved in with a woman whom he was dating whom she didn't approve of. She was surprised to realize that she felt like this woman had replaced her. She had attached her identity and personal happiness to her son. She often would make her son choose between her and his girlfriend by threatening to cut him off if he stayed with his girlfriend or by not supporting him financially if he didn't drop everything and come to her rescue. Unconsciously, she had made him the "man of the house" as a single mother since she had no other significant male energy in her life. He was the only man in her life. I asked her why she made it all about the other woman when, in actuality, the issue was within herself.

When Letting Go it is important to:

- Know that letting him leave your care is natural and necessary
- Establish new boundaries that support his freedom as an adult
- Respect your son's decision even when you don't agree
- Recognize your feelings of loss
- Pray for your son

Reflection Questions

Letting go involves "loosening the reigns" and trusting your maturing son to demonstrate that he can handle more responsibility.

1. How can you create new expectations that reflect your "loosening of the reigns?"
2. How can you give advice without influencing his decision?

Getting Your son "off of your breast"

After setting boundaries and letting go, the next steps are to re-establish mutual respect, recognize him as an adult, and be purposeful about scheduling quality time together. These actions may take the form of:

1. not butting into his personal relationships, but instead offering advice, when requested.
2. not rushing to bail him out but allowing him to problem solve.
3. making well-informed decisions before giving him money.
4. having him honor your personal space.
5. disciplining him or rendering consequences when a violation has occurred.

By not weaning our sons, continuing to "baby" them, and "keeping them on our breast" can cause our sons to stay dependent on us, or handicap their emotional development, and in turn, be dependent on other women, long after they should be able to stand on their own two feet. A son then doesn't learn how to take care of himself. This can turn into resentment towards his mother later in life as she attempts to wean him as an adult. The adult son then uses threats and volatile behavior to get his way. On one hand, he desires to be self-sufficient, and self-determined, but he can become spoiled and dependent upon her constant "breast milk."

Recognizing this is essential to creating a new, healthier relationship. Mothers have to fight the urge to rescue "their baby" and instead allow him to grow through and learn from his own mistakes. A healthy relationship will cause both the mother and son to grow. She gets to learn how to set and stick to boundaries, and the older he gets, he learns how to become increasingly self-supporting, self-sufficient, a critical thinker, independent, less dependent, and reliance upon his mother.

A mother I met with struggled with creating a new healthier relationship with her eighteen-year-old son in whom she disapproved of his living situation. She felt those he lived with were a bad influence. Because of this she couldn't accept him nor his new lifestyle. She wanted to reject him and forgo a relationship with him until he changed his behavior and moved back in with her.

I challenged her to create a healthy relationship with him without criticizing his friends and his current living arrangement. She was resistant because she didn't want him to think she approved of his lifestyle. She thought by rejecting him, it would force him into doing what she wanted him to do. Unfortunately, this wasn't working. Because she rejected him, she was miserable and constantly worried about him. So she accepted the challenge and started to creating a new relationship with him by establishing several new commitments for herself. These boundaries started off simple; committing to talk at least once a week so she knew he was safe, not giving him money to bail him out of consequences based on his behavior and not bringing up his living situation. Now she talks to him consistently and he is starting to communicate with her about his disappointment with his recent decisions. These are the questions I asked her to answer:

1. What about his behavior was upsetting you?
2. How can you express your concerns without attacking him?
3. What does your son need from you now?
4. What do you need to feel at ease and peace with his decision(s)?
5. What do you want going forward?

Reflection

I know that it can be difficult and scary to let your son go. Trust what you've instilled in him. I believe your son will surprise you when you cease the criticism and allow him to mature into a healthy adult. Be sure to keep the doors of communication open so he knows he can talk to you when he needs support.

Chapter 8

Life after Loss

On March 29, 2013 at 7:29pm, I received the dreaded phone call that no parent *ever* wants to receive. *"They shot him!"* said the hysterical voice on the other end of the phone line. The "him" they were talking about was my son, KB. I was in disbelief, in shock. After placing a call to my sister and his biological father, I arrived at the hospital. While sitting in the waiting room I kept telling myself, "Maybe, he only got shot in the leg." "And *of course* he's going to survive." When the doctor finally entered the waiting room after 20 minutes, she said the words I'll never forget, "He lost a lot of blood. We tried everything we could, but unfortunately, he didn't make it." I slid down the wall and fell to the ground, in a daze. I could hear screaming, chaos, and someone beating the wall. It was the sound of one of KB's friends pounding the wall in disbelief and shock. Hoping it was all a nightmare and not real I opened my eyes and saw the hand of the doctor extended toward me. I grabbed it and she walked me to the room where my only child, my 19-year-old son K'Breyan Clark was lying dead of a gunshot wound to his neck.

The next few months would be filled with pain, despair, depression, anger, hopelessness, and extreme sadness. While brushing my teeth one morning six months after KB's death, I heard the Holy Spirit whisper these words to me: *"Don't die with him."* This was a turning point for me. I had to face the truth that my son wasn't away on vacation, spending the night at a friend's house or off at a summer basketball camp. I had to come to grips with the fact that I would never see him alive again. No matter how long I waited at the door, he wasn't going to turn that knob and walk in.

Six months after his death, I made the decision not to die with my son - I made a decision to LIVE! It was this decision that restored my hope, got me out of the bed, and gave me the resolve to leave my secure 20-year, six-figure management job and start my coaching and speaking business. Even writing this book is the result of that decision. Because of this resolve, I have been on a mission to help women break free from fear, negative mindsets, and self-sabotaging behaviors so they can achieve the greatness they desire and deserve. I chose to turn my pain into passion and let my emotions fuel my purpose.

Looking back at the last five years of my son's life, I can't help but to reflect on all the time I wasted being angry, depressed, living beneath my purpose, people pleasing, being fearful, and constantly disappointed with myself. I wasted too much time not enjoying the moments I had with him, pushing him away and wanting him to be somebody he wasn't.

Slaying the Regret Monster

As with any loss, it is natural to experience regret. The feelings of regret overtook me and would constantly consume my daily thoughts. Soon, I was weighed down with guilt to the point where I could no longer function. Every time the emotion of regret came up, it won. My mind would almost instantly go to an incident where I wasn't at my best as a parent, and instantly I would feel guilty. I had so many regrets to come to grips with:

> I regretted not having a lot of pictures of the two of us together,
>
> I regretted not listening to my husband's advice,
>
> I regretted the times I yelled for nothing,
>
> I regretted the times I ignored him,
>
> I regretted the times I sat him in front of the TV screen and pushed repeat on the VCR to be entertained by kiddie videos, over and over, so that I could have some "me" time,
>
> I regretted not taking more family vacations,
>
> I regretted missing any of his basketball games,
>
> I regretted not saying, "I Love You" the last time I spoke to him,
>
> I regretted not teaching him more responsibility,
>
> I regretted not listening to him more, and

I regretted not being the mother he needed me to be.

It became apparent that until I dealt with the feeling of regret they would constantly keep showing up and haunting me. Each time Regret reared its ugly head, I learned to replace it with a positive memory of my son. I told myself that my son knew he was loved and I expressed my gratitude for the time we had together.

I got my journal and wrote down at least one thought of gratitude towards my son. I said it out loud and I took it in with two deep breaths. I did this simple gratitude exercise every day for the next 30 days. Doing this not only brought back great memories of my son, the exercise gave me over 30 weapons to use to slay the Regret monster. I share this same strategy with my clients to assist them in slaying their Regret monster.

What Regret Monsters do you need to slay? List them.

_____

_____

_____

Challenge

Do the 30-day Gratitude Exercise above to help you "Slay the Regret Monster."

Celebrating the Good

To overcome the constant feelings of guilt and regret, I had to learn to recall and celebrate the good times we had together and all the great things about my son. What I find most interesting is that all of memories I now have of my son are good. My love for him doesn't allow me to experience anything else. These memories are separate from my emotions. I believe this is what the love of God is like - having the ability to separate who a person is from what they've done. This is so important to practice with our living sons. Don't lose sight of celebrating what's good about him. It can be very hard to separate the behavior from the person, especially when your son is misbehaving, but it is critical for him to know that he is loved even though he's made mistakes. Most importantly, he needs to know that his mistakes don't have to define who he is.

Often when we are in the throes of dealing with their rebellion, all they hear from us is criticism, judgment, condemnation, complaint and disappointment. If we dwell on the mistakes, he will grow to believe he is hopeless and powerless to change his outcome. Instead this is an opportunity for us to inspire, motivate and activate their inner greatness. Emphasize the positive things they are doing and allow them to outshine the negative ones. This will help him recognize his potential and ability to do well and to overcome his mistakes.

Honoring our Sons

Since his death, I refuse to speak ill of my son or his behaviors. He will not be remembered by what he did but by who he was as a person, how he made me feel, how he lit up a room, how resilient he was, and how his smile made my day. I spend time talking about him with his friends in honor of his memory. Because he was only nineteen years old, I want to make sure his time on this earth is remembered positively. I don't pretend he was the model citizen but I don't attach judgment to his behaviors. His short life was full of love, excitement, high energy, traveling, loads of fun, laughter, family and friends.

Death has so many lessons to teach the living: to live, to love, to celebrate, and to honor life. KB lived and loved hard. He was vibrant and full of life. He was the life of the party and boy, could he light up a room. I now have resolved not to allow his death to kill me or my purpose. I honor him by resolving every day to live fully, to enjoy life and to live on purpose.

Honoring our sons in a society that clearly doesn't value them is necessary. Honor your son by supporting his dreams; by looking for, speaking on, and celebrating the good; by challenging him, by loving him even when you don't like him, and by allowing him to grow from and through his mistakes.

Reflection

No matter what the condition is of the relationship you have with your son, I urge you to celebrate the fact that he is alive by loving him and honoring him.

Reflection Questions

1. List 3-5 things to celebrate/honor your son.
2. Bake a cake or make his favorite meal to celebrate him. Make it a point to give him the specific reasons you are celebrating him.
3. How can you show your son that you value him?
4. Tell your son a specific reason why he is important to you.

To Mothers Raising Sons

Chapter 9

The Struggle

The Struggle is Real

As much as I have decided to live my life there is still the ever-present internal fight to want to succumb to depression and despair. Even now, I sometimes find myself wanting to stay in the bed, cry myself to sleep, and give up more often than I want to admit. Accepting the fact that I'll never see my son on this side of heaven is one of the hardest things I've ever had to face. There are days when it feels like a bad dream. The struggle is real.

The struggle to live despite my broken heart, my disappointment, and my anger is real. Even on my best days, the struggle is real. The struggle is to get out of the bed, to go to sleep, to eat, to stop eating junk food, to honor my body, to get out and engage with others, to keep moving forward, to encourage others, to pray, to not succumb to guilt, to not seek revenge, to not be enraged about his unsolved murder, to continue to believe God, and to keep doing my forgiveness work – it is all very REAL.

Mothers who have lost their sons to drugs, prison, abandonment, jail, gangs, mental illness, and disability also experience this struggle. The struggle is to fight against what is happening in us, and the work required for us to become our highest self. Part of what keeps us struggling internally is the constant, plaguing question, *"Why did this happen to me?"*

The struggle is *not* to stay in hurt and to *not* forego accepting the greater assignment to allow the loss to uncover my purpose, to develop my character, to expand my thinking and to grow me. It may seem easier to stay broken, angry and wounded, become bitter, to just let life happen around you and to wear your pain as a badge or as an excuse to stay stuck. I get it - there is a constant inclination within to stay the victim and to lose myself in the heart wrenching pain. My intention, on a daily basis, is to rise, heal a little bit more each day, and to use my pain as a catalyst for others' great awakening. This great awakening comes about as you and I begin to face the pain and start the healing process.

Guilt about moving forward

One of the struggles I still have is knowing I have to move forward, and the guilt that is associated with moving forward. I feel guilty if I move forward too quickly, thinking that moving forward too quickly means that I'm not honoring my son's death, or that somehow I'm betraying him. In a way, I also have moments of believing that moving forward is a reflection of my lack of love for him. The thought of moving forward can bring up feelings of guilt that try to convince me that I'm betraying my son or turning my back on him by experiencing joy or trying to move onward and upward. The guilt causes me to question whether moving forward will somehow make him mad, will he think I didn't love him, what will others think, what is an appropriate time to move forward and am I benefitting from his death by using it as an opportunity for attention or a spotlight?

As mentioned earlier, the struggle is whether to allow this guilt to bind me or hinder me, or propel me and keep me moving forward. I choose to believe that moving forward honors my son, allows me to heal, and converts my pain into the passion needed to fulfill my life assignment to support other mothers of sons.

Overcoming the Desire to Stay in the Pain

One of the easiest things to do is to stay in the pain. It is natural for me to feel the heart-wrenching pain, to cry uncontrollably, to complain how unfair it is and to scream at the top of my lungs. I have the best excuses to stay hurt and to stay in pain. No one would dare argue about the amount of pain a mother who had to bury her child is enduring and her reason for staying right there in the midst of her brokenness. There are those who can't imagine how I'm able to go forward living my life. For others, just the thought of losing their child sends them reeling in heartache. I could easily justify why I don't participate in some activities, go certain places and why I don't attend funerals. I can stay right in this pain and most people would be just fine with that, and times I would be too.

I've watched this play out numerous times - people avoiding me because they don't know what to say. Or you can feel like they are moving on without you, leaving you behind, stuck in your pain. Those that do speak up, with their best intentions, may tell you to move on, that time will heal your wound, tell you how strong you are and how they wouldn't survive if it was their son that was killed. It is rare to find someone who will sit with you and let you cry uncontrollably without uttering a word. So what I did was avoid conversations about my son after his death. I stopped the tears from flowing when I was around other people and I carried on as if I was ok, even when deep down inside, I felt like I was dying.

I now consider pain an invitation for me to fight for my very life. My life didn't end with my son's death and neither did my higher calling and life assignment. When I feel the pain, it serves as a reminder of my decision and declaration to live, of the gift I was blessed with for nineteen years, and the life assignment that is greater than me.

I recall at his funeral a pastor told me to bury everything with my son that day. I'll never forget that advice and I did just that. After the funeral, I set out on a mission to bury every dead thing in my life. That same mission led me to where I am today. This pain has caused me to do an inventory of my life and to let go of what no longer serves me, including beliefs that I am not good enough, not lovable and was a bad parent. In some cases, I've let go of certain friendships and associates that no longer align with who I am now. And I've let go of suppressing my feelings and silencing my voice.

Staying in pain is no longer an option for me. The pain is real and the pain is there but I have made a conscious choice not to allow the pain to overtake me nor my purpose. If I stay in pain, I will miss the opportunity to help another mother save her son. I will miss the opportunity to enjoy my husband, my family, and friends and those connected to me. I will miss living. Now I resolve to:

1. Lean into my pain, embrace it, and not run away from it.
2. Allow myself to feel it so that I can heal from it.
3. Use my pain to uncover beliefs and past hurts that need to be addressed.
4. Turn my pain into lessons that support my spiritual growth.
5. Share my lessons to help others heal.

As it relates to helping and supporting other mothers of sons, I now resolve:

1. Not to judge them.
2. To share my story with them.
3. Be a listening ear.
4. Provide a safe space for them to be vulnerable.
5. Help them heal and help them connect to the resources they need.

Reflection Exercise

List 5 personal resolves that are a result of the pain or parenting struggles you've experienced with your son

1._____

2._____

3._____

4._____

5._____

Making peace

As I sat upright in my bed after leaving the hospital earlier that fateful day, reality began setting in. I asked, *"Why did this happen, God!?"* This was the question that plagued me. I yelled it, I scream it, I cried it, I wrote it, I thought it, and I whispered it! I was so mad at God! I had attended church regularly; served in almost every capacity in my church. At church I was the "model" Christian. I was even an ordained minister. It was difficult to admit that I was mad at God. I was so faithful so, "Why me God? Why did You have to allow *my* child to be taken?"

    I felt like everything I believed was in question. I thought, beyond a shadow of doubt, that my son would live a long life. How could I continue to preach about a loving God that hears and answers our prayers and who protects His children when my belief was wavering? What had I done to deserve this fate? Where did I go wrong? Was I being punished? These questions haunted me and kept me in turmoil.

When I wasn't mad at God, I was mad at those who senselessly took my child's life. Why hadn't they been caught yet? Are the detectives really investigating? How is it that they could get away with such a callous act? This made me even angrier at God. Wasn't it enough that he was murdered? And now it seemed the murderers were getting away with it? *Are you serious, God?*

It is important for you to know that it is common to blame God for a child's death. We somehow believe that a loving God wouldn't take our child. The truth is He didn't. God didn't do this to him or to me. I wasn't being punished nor was he. His death was a consequence of someone else exercising their free will, and maybe even of KB exercising his, in the choices he made. God gives to all of us free will. His death was a result of free will. I had to accept this and understand that this wasn't about me. My son had his own life and the ability to use the same free will I had, as did his murderer.

Making peace was more about me seeking God with the intent to understand how He could use my pain for a greater purpose than understanding why the murder happened. Making peace required me to surrender the need to stay in my feelings and to understand how to keep living despite the pain. In finding peace with the death of my only child I had to find peace within myself. This meant me choosing to let go of wanting to wear my pain like a badge, refusing to heal and staying in the bed, in a depression. Peace required me to give up my pre-conceived notions of what my life should look like and to accept that something larger and greater that could occur if I accepted God's invitation to use my story to help other mothers heal from their past wounds and to support them as they navigated trying to raise their sons.

Making peace is letting go of the need to be right, justified, and validated. Peace is the absence of hostility and an agreement to end inner conflict and struggle. I wanted to end the hostility I had with God and myself, so I decided to make peace. Making peace was the result of my decision to release my feelings of hostility towards God, myself, my son, and my parents and exchange it for peaceful emotions such as love, worthiness, and acceptance, which supported my healing.

Reflection Exercise

Step 1 – Answer the following questions

1. What or Who am I allowing to disturb my peace?
2. What emotions am I experiencing as a result of this hostility?
3. What could happen if I stay in hostility?
4. What is possible if I release the hostility?

Step 2 - A Divine Exchange.
This exercise will help you release unhealthy emotions that are causing you hostility and exchange them for more peaceful emotions.

Hostility (list the emotions that are causing you hostility)		Peace (list the emotions to replace hostility with peace)
I trade in my **ANGER**	for	**JOY**
	for	
	for	
	for	
	for	
	for	
	for	

Step 3 - After completing the table, write each emotion on a separate piece of paper. Make two stacks Hostility (on the left) and Peace (on the right) in order of the sentences above. Have a small bag, trash can or basket on hand.

Step 4 - Grab the pieces of paper, in sequence, one by one, from the Hostility stack, hold it in your hand and say out loud, I trade in my (fill in the blank), for (fill in the blank- what's written on the piece of paper from the Peace stack) and drop the paper while picking up that paper from the stack. Repeat until all exchanges have been made.

Step 5 – Burn the Hostility papers

The purpose of burning the papers is to symbolize a permanent letting go or release. Allow yourself to feel the emotions as they burn and as you see them disintegrating let your mind release them.

Step 6 - Write an Inner Peace Treaty with yourself. This treaty is your declaration of peace. It should include what you will do to guard your peace. Use this as a daily affirmation or hang it somewhere prominent as a reminder of the commitment you made with yourself to release hostility.

Triumph

A few months after burying my son, I attended a retreat at the home of Dr. Maxine Mimms, my mentor's mentor. She asked me about myself and in response I shared with her that my only son had been murdered. What she then shared with was full of glorious wisdom, *"What happened was indeed tragic, but what would be a tragedy is if you did nothing with it."* She went on to say, *"What are you going to do with your pain?"* This question pierced my heart and had me in deep reflection that entire weekend and the weeks that followed. *What was I going to do with my pain?*

The space I'd been in was wanting to stay mired in the pain, mourning for the rest of my days on the earth. I wanted to blame God and keep my back turned to Him. I wanted to run away and hide under the covers. But this mighty woman's question wouldn't leave me alone. It followed me around until I answered. One day, while lying on the floor of my bedroom, crying uncontrollably, banging my fists on the floor and screaming out in utter despair for what seemed like hours, I decided to give my pain to God. In that moment, I gave up trying to figure it out, and trying to determine why and how this could happen to me. And I surrendered my pain using the process below.

I had come to place where I could no longer hold the pain. I gave it to God as an offering. I gave my pain over to God. I thought if anyone knew what to do with it, God did. I opened my mouth and begin to name my pain *out loud*, my heartbreak, my despair, my emptiness, and my hurt. I closed my eyes, I allowed myself to feel every emotion as I named each one out loud. I made the motions of gathering them all placing them in both hands, I fell to my knees, I lifted my hands full of my pain and with all my being I said, *"I give each one to you. I cast them onto you as an offering. I ask you to take them, take them from my heart, my mind and my spirit. I lay them at the feet of the altar, Lord. I replace them with love, peace and wisdom. I have faith that you will turn them into something that I can use."* Each time the pain comes creeping back I repeat the same process. I choose to feel whole and I have faith that God will recycle and repurpose my pain.

After I gave my pain to God I started asking a different type of question: *"How can You use my pain for good? How can I use this pain to bring You glory, and to help others?"* Six months later I started a support group for mothers who lost their sons to gun violence, and I used my pain and experience to create workshops to help those experiencing painful circumstances titled, "Turning Tragedy into Triumph" and "Surviving the Storm." In helping others, I began to heal. My pain started working for my good and I started to see how my pain could fuel a greater purpose. The very thing that came to break me starting making me whole.

The pain also became my greatest teacher, exposing areas in my life that were weak and needed to be rebuilt and reinforced. These areas included exposing true feelings I'd hidden and suppressed, how I had silenced my voice for fear of rejection, and the unresolved and unhealed places within me where I harbored resentment towards my parents that had spilled over in other relationships.

My new commitment required me to get aligned with who I was designed and created to be. This meant I had to get free from insecurity, feelings of inadequacy and people pleasing. I could no longer operate the ways I had prior to KB's death: playing small, paralyzed by fear, and only going half way. My pain was used to fuel my passion to help women heal and train up their Black boys, to coach women through their pain, and to walk in total freedom in all areas of their lives. My pain gave me the courage to release my attachment to material things, and the old jealousy and competitive inner attitude that had me feel the need to keep up with the Jones' began to fall away.

From Pain to Purpose

Pain can reveal our greater purpose, if we let it. Purpose is using your pain to serve others. Pain helps us connect with others who have or are currently experiencing pain like or similar to ours. It allows us to see others past their outer shell and invites us to meet them at the place of their pain or struggle. Pain can also act like a spiritual laser beam, blasting away the crust and exposing years of accumulated bitterness. We then can transform the pain and make space in our hearts to extend love and compassion to others. Pain can also help you recognize how very connected we each are as human beings, and how knitted together we truly are through our shared human experience. The connection can then serve as a common platform upon which both of us can heal, and begin living even more purposefully. Living in our purpose wakes us up in the morning, motivates, and pushes us to live through another day, and gives us the strength needed to stay in the fight. This purpose becomes our guiding light and keeps us focused even when pain strikes again. And when we attach those we are called to serve to our purpose, we then have the accountability to keep going when we feel like quitting or giving up.

The purpose revealed for our lives is the very reason we are here in this earth at this present time. If we allow ourselves to stay in the pain, we essentially stay stuck in the past. We will never move forward into the present time which is where our purpose awaits us. Staying in the pain keeps us living in a time that no longer exists, with our eyes focused on our life's rear-view mirror, which is only filled with sad memories, fantasies, regrets, "would haves" and "should haves." The danger of staying here is that you are powerless to change the past, but you are not powerless to learn from it. Your power resides in the present. It isn't time that heals, it is living in the present time that does. Living in the present doesn't ignore the past but instead uses its lessons to inform us, grow us, and make us wiser. We then can gain a better of understanding of the precious, limited time we have been given to walk out our purpose.

I have the audacity to believe God when He says in Genesis 50:20a, "What was meant for evil He will turn into good" and I was determined to find the Good in this tragic situation. I sought Him until I found Him and I didn't give up until my purpose was revealed.

I refuse to stay in pain and I refuse to allow the pain to win.

*What will you do with **your** pain?*

Chapter 10

Moving Forward

Loving Again

Honestly speaking, the idea of moving forward scared me. How could I live without my son? He was my reason for living; he was my first love. I was sure that he would outlive me. I wasn't prepared to bury my child and to face life without him. But I had to continue to love and live for my husband, my grandson and most importantly, myself. In surrendering my pain to God, I learned that lives were attached to me and that if I chose to die, I would miss an opportunity to help those suffering through what I had for so many years. It was this truth that gave me the courage to face myself and to allow God to transform me so that I could walk out my purpose in this earth.

It was my search for love that brought me to where I am today both spiritually and physically. But in order for me to live again and love again, I fully had to heal, be restored, and also *be made whole*. One of the first messages I received from God after KB's death was that I needed be healed and also made whole. Being healed involved the restoration of my heart from the constant hurting and pain. Being made whole meant that my mind, body and spirit would be in full alignment with who I was created to be. Being whole also meant that I didn't need another's love or acceptance of me in order to have an experience of love. Being whole meant accepting that I am loved, lovable, and loving myself by having my mind restored to the truth of Who I Am.

I now can love from a place of power and not a place of fear. Loving again wasn't something I thought was possible for myself. My "M. O." was to shut down and stay angry - but God had other plans for me and my life. Loving again meant opening my heart again without fear of rejection or abandonment.

I chose love when the circumstances of my life would have wanted me to hate.

I choose to spend my time celebrating stead of lamenting my son's life, replacing hate with love.

I choose to paint my memories with love and not regret.

I choose to remember his love for me and not the times I felt abandoned by him.

I CHOOSE LOVE.

I CHOOSE LOVE.

Love is what is sustaining and keeping me. Loving again is a conscious, DAILY, deliberate, intentional decision to re-open my heart, to love fully, to trust others and to receive love.

Living Again

While standing over my son's casket, all of me wanted to jump in and be buried with my son. It was at that very moment, looking down at his lifeless body, that I decided to live and to not die with him. It was at that moment that the life I knew before his death would be changed forever. Standing at that casket I saw where I had not been fully living but had been merely existing. I saw myself hitting the snooze button, dreading going to a job where I was unfulfilled, I saw relationships that weren't reciprocal and activities I had participated in that didn't bring me joy. I walked away from the casket to become a new person.

I decided it was my time to live and to live more *fully*. For so many years I played it safe. I had a good job, owned a home, attended church regularly, and had a husband. I had big dreams of starting my own business, leaving my job and traveling the world but I never had the courage to do anything with those dreams. At that casket, I realized how short life is and how unpredictable it is and I decided to address every one of the unhealed areas in my life. If I didn't, I would be among the many "walking dead," walking around frustrated, not satisfied with life and pretending to be happy. I didn't want that for myself. I wanted real happiness, not pretend happiness.

To Mothers Raising Sons

From My Heart to Yours –

For Mothers Raising Black Boys

The pain of losing a child is a pain I can't describe and wouldn't desire for anyone. The pain is both unbearable and unimaginable. It is my prayer that you first and foremost recognize your son as a gift and your very reward from God. God blessed you with a son. As a mother you were given the divine role to develop his maturity and emotional resiliency so that he could withstand life's challenges, disappointment, hurt and rejection. The only way you can be successful in doing this is if you are healed and whole. It is literally a life or death matter that you do the "inner work" so that your parenting is not based in your own unhealed wounds and hurts. When you are healed and whole, what you impart to your son bears "good fruit." I know, at times it may seem impossible to get his attention and to influence his decisions but you undeniably have an impact on him, whether it's done knowingly or unknowingly. You absolutely matter and are invaluable to him and his life.

I understand that there may or may not be valid reasons for why his father isn't in his life, if that is the case, I urge you to examine yourself. If it's because of you, or if it's because your own emotional wounds or resentment or bitterness towards the father is causing you to interfere with his presence in your son's life, then I urge you to get the help you need to forgive, heal and move on so that your son can have a relationship with his father. When your son doesn't have a relationship with his father, it can turn into anger and rage, that left unattended, can lead to violence, bad behavior, low self-esteem, and low self-confidence as he gets older. If his father isn't interested in a relationship with him, I ask you to find positive male role models who can teach, guide and mentor him.

I pray that my story and my pain will spare you from the tragedy of losing your son to death, drugs, hopelessness, the streets, jail, a gang, or destruction. I invite you to be the mother and not the friend, to use your struggles to teach him resilience, to teach him to use his creativity, critical thinking skills, and to use his mistakes to teach him discipline and determination. I invite you not to treat him like he is your man but to be the parent. Give him challenges that will spur growth in his character and spirit. He needs you to help teach him responsibility, the value of earning his own money, the consequences of not following your rules, to respect himself and others, to be morally upstanding, to express himself in healthy ways, and how to love unconditionally. Believe me, this will help him become a responsible, fulfilled adult.

Lastly, I want you to savor each moment with him as a gift and be determined not to waste any more time screaming, crying, debating, and fighting with him. Instead cherish the time you have with him and recognize your assignment: to develop your son into a stable, grounded, disciplined, well-adjusted and successful man.

Epilogue

Nova

You were my sunshine, my son; my divine in day's light, even at night's time: with the stars, you shine. Now it's stormy, dark clouds are raining, pouring blurry and hurried. I am worried: Did my bedtime stories chase your nightmares through the perennial, celestial bright lights to guide you into heaven for the rest of your life?

You've been chosen – so soon – now I see you anew, in the face of the full moons and the early morning's dew and the sun's shining light in the afternoons.

He chose you so soon. There's nothing I could say or do. Just be happy. You are still my sunshine, my divine, in day's light, even night's time among the stars-you are my nova. I am happy I know where you are: that brightest star up there. And I know now my bedtime stories did not chase you into my stormy nightmare.

For KB 03/29/16

Written by Cynthia Warren Clark (Kathei's mother, KB's grandmother)

Connecting with the Kathei

Connect with her via her website

http://coachkathei.com

Connect with her via email

conact@coachkathei.com

Connect with her via phone

(253) 642-7228

Connect with her via social media

Facebook: http://facebook.com/coachkathei

Instragram: coachkathei

Twitter: @coachkathei

Offerings:

Freedom Coaching – one on one coaching to help you uncover any faulty beliefs that you may be unconsciously operating under.

Public Speaking – can speak on topics relating to the importance of inner healing work and mothering, mothers raising sons and how to parent from a healthy place. I also can provide customized workshops for groups, associations, and organizations.

References

1. Clinton, T. & Sibcy. G. (2006) "Loving Your Child Too Much," Franklin, Tennessee: Integrity Publishers.

2. Erwin, C.L. (2006) "The Everything Parent's Guide To Raising Boys: A Complete Handbook to Develop Confidence, Promote Self-esteem, And Improve Communication," Avon, Massachusetts: Adams Media

www.ingramcontent.com/pod-product-compliance
Lightning Source LLC
LaVergne TN
LVHW051602070426
835507LV00021B/2712